SERENDIP

SERENDIP
MY SRI LANKAN KITCHEN

Peter Kuruvita

PHOTOGRAPHY BY ALAN BENSON
AND PHILIP KURUVITA

murdoch books
Sydney | London

Contents

Preface

THE HEART OF EVERY SRI LANKAN HOUSE IS ITS KITCHEN AND THAT IS THE ROOM I HAVE ALWAYS BEEN DRAWN TO.

In January 2007, at a literary festival in Galle, I overheard some local women talking about the lack of good reference books for Sri Lankan curries. Thus inspired, and yearning to revisit childhood memories, I set out to write this book.

I started returning to Sri Lanka on a regular basis, visiting numerous kitchens in my search for recipes. It quickly became clear that many were easier to find than I had anticipated—they were right there in Dehiwala, our family's ancestral home. Once I had my recipes, I went to the markets with my cousin Manori, then organised a major cook-off with all the ladies of the Kuruvita clan. It was the first time in years they had been together like this and, just as in the old days, they still argued about every single dish. One of the wonderful things about all Sri Lankans and their food is that they rarely agree on the details of any recipe. Most are handed down through generations and include their own very special preparation methods and flavours. I hope I have captured the most treasured recipes from my family's kitchen, and I also hope this collection encourages other Sri Lankans living far from home to get back into their kitchens and share our rich, diverse culinary tradition with their families and friends.

As well as mining my family's kitchen history, I have also sought out other authentic recipes for a range of Sri Lanka's best-loved and most traditional dishes. In Sri Lanka, people will travel kilometres for the perfect egg hopper, for example, or coconut sambal. Some of the tastiest meals are still bought from small roadside stalls and 'boutiques'—most of which are simple little shacks.

These are the recipes I wish to share with you.

Peter Kuruvita, Sydney 2008

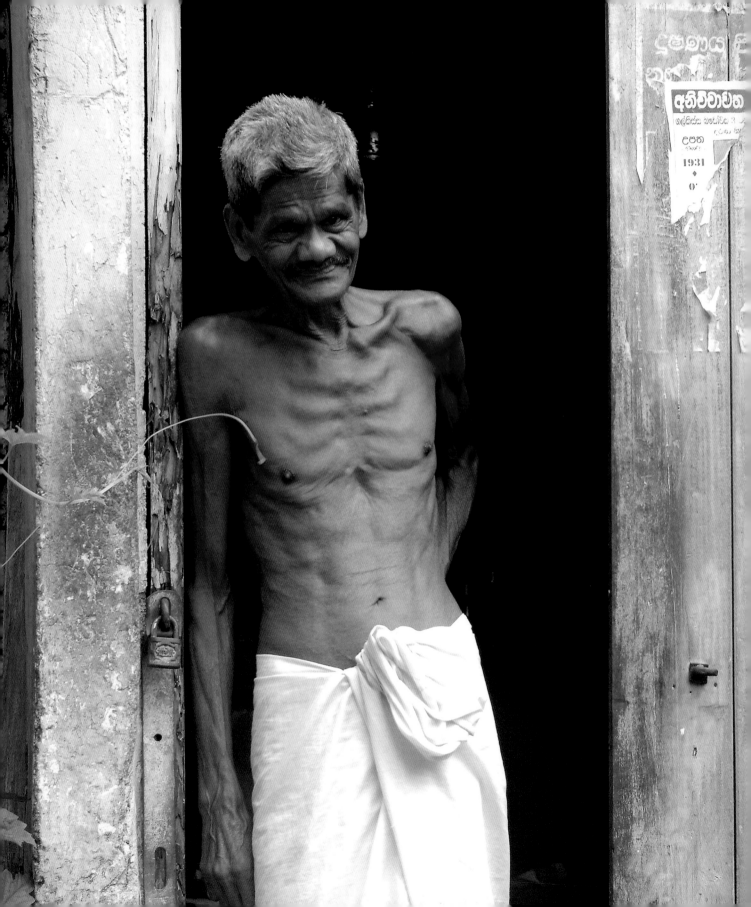

Introduction

MY SRI LANKAN STORY BEGINS WITH ME STANDING ON THE VERY TIP
OF SOUTHERN INDIA, STUNNED, BECAUSE DAD WAS ABOUT TO TRY AND
JUMP OUR PRECIOUS AUSTIN MINIBUS (CONTAINING EVERYTHING WE
OWNED) OFF A RICKETY WHARF ONTO TWO LINKED DUGOUT CANOES.
THIS STRANGE BARGE WAS TO BE PADDLED OUT TO A FERRY AND OUR
MINIBUS HOISTED LIKE A COW ONTO THE SRI LANKA-BOUND VESSEL.
I WAS FOUR-AND-A-HALF YEARS OLD.

We had already driven the minibus from the UK across France, Germany, Austria,
Yugoslavia, Bulgaria, Turkey, Iran, Pakistan and India. Our arrival in Sri Lanka
would mark the return of the prodigal son, Wickramapala Kuruvita—my father—
who had left home on his Indian motorcycle many years earlier to seek his
fortune in England.

It must have been quite a sight: five-and-a-half of us packed into an Austin
minibus—Dad, my Austrian mother, Liselotte Katharina, me, my eight-year-old
brother Philip and, at the last minute, a Sri Lankan cousin who wanted to come
along for the ride. The 'half' was my unborn brother, David Sangeeva—Mum was
four months pregnant when we set out from the UK.

Our family's journey began in London in February 1968 and was due to be
completed seven weeks later. Dad, the head of the London 'house of Kuruvita', had
nursed the concept of this daring expedition for a long time. Now, after closing his
business in London, his plan was to take the family overland to his hometown of
Dehiwala, just outside the boundaries of Colombo. We all trusted in Dad's ability
to pull us through any difficulties, and so his dream became reality.

The excitement of preparation was great. Dad charmed Lord Primrose (who was thirteenth in line to the British throne but preferred to do his own thing in a workshop close to Dad's) into selling him the almost new Austin minibus for 20 pounds.

But because Mum was pregnant, Dad was worried about her undertaking the trip; he suggested she take a plane instead of risking her own and the baby's life in the middle of some wilderness. This was completely unacceptable to Mum—how could she possibly forgo such an adventure? In the end Dad agreed, but found an insurance policy that would fly her 'home' should she need evacuation; he craftily worded the document in such a way that 'home' could mean London or Colombo.

The British Automobile Association provided detailed information on road conditions, distances, sights of particular interest and places where we could buy petrol en route. Eleven countries, three ferries and roughly 20,000 kilometres would be involved if we were to accomplish this journey. We had to drive through snow and ice, over mountains and deserts, and finally through the unforgiving heat of the dry season in India. Forty-one degrees Celsius in the shade made Dad decide to drive day and night to get to our destination one week earlier than planned.

After a visit to the 400-year-old temple at Madurai in southern India we were informed that Danushkodi could only be reached by train; and the minibus had to be loaded too. From Danushkodi, a ferry would take us across to Sri Lanka.

Danushkodi was a desolate, sandy outpost with only a large cadjan shed, thatched with coconut leaves, housing the immigration and customs officers. There were long queues stretching out over the white sand. The seafront was cordoned off and the ferry was only just visible more than a kilometre out from the shore. Dad stood all morning in the burning sun trying to clear our passage, only to be told that it was impossible to take the minibus to the ferry: the last cyclone had washed away the pier. The next available port was Bombay, about 1400 kilometres away.

The best time for Dad's particular genius to spring forth was when a situation became desperate. He asked us to stay put, and disappeared. Not long after, he returned with the owners of two dugout fishing canoes, showed them how to tie their flimsy craft together, and paid for some of the ferry's cargo nets to be spread

out on special wooden blocks on top of the newly created 'barge'. By that time a huge crowd had secured a premier place on the beach to see what spectacle would unfold. My mother gasped—she realised what he intended to do and was frightened. Only that morning we had experienced the quicksand on the shores when we drove closer to the water to cool off. Some kind villagers had come to the rescue and helped to dig out the wheels. What would happen this time?

We children were quiet, and everyone held their breath as Dad lined up our vehicle, accelerated to skim over the top of the treacherous sandy surface and landed with screeching brakes precisely on the two little canoes. He had to wait three hours for the tides to be right before a tugboat was able to pull him and his eccentric rig across a stretch of sea to meet the ferry.

Meanwhile, one small group at a time, all the other passengers boarded an old, wobbly sailing boat hauled by a tug, which took them out to the ferry. By the time Dad's strange procession came alongside, we were all standing on the ferry's upper deck watching. The ship's crane reached out and secured the minibus, ready to hoist it onto the cargo deck. Precariously balanced, it suddenly slipped, dangling halfway between the sea and the safety of the deck. I had asked to be picked up so I could see better, but when it looked as if the minibus was about to fall back into the sea I became hysterical, shouting 'Daddy, Daddy, my Daddy!' I thought Dad was still in the minibus. With typical Wickramapala aplomb he appeared behind us, the minibus was successfully stowed on board and the ferry was able to set off.

We finally arrived in Sri Lanka exhausted but safe.

Meet
my family

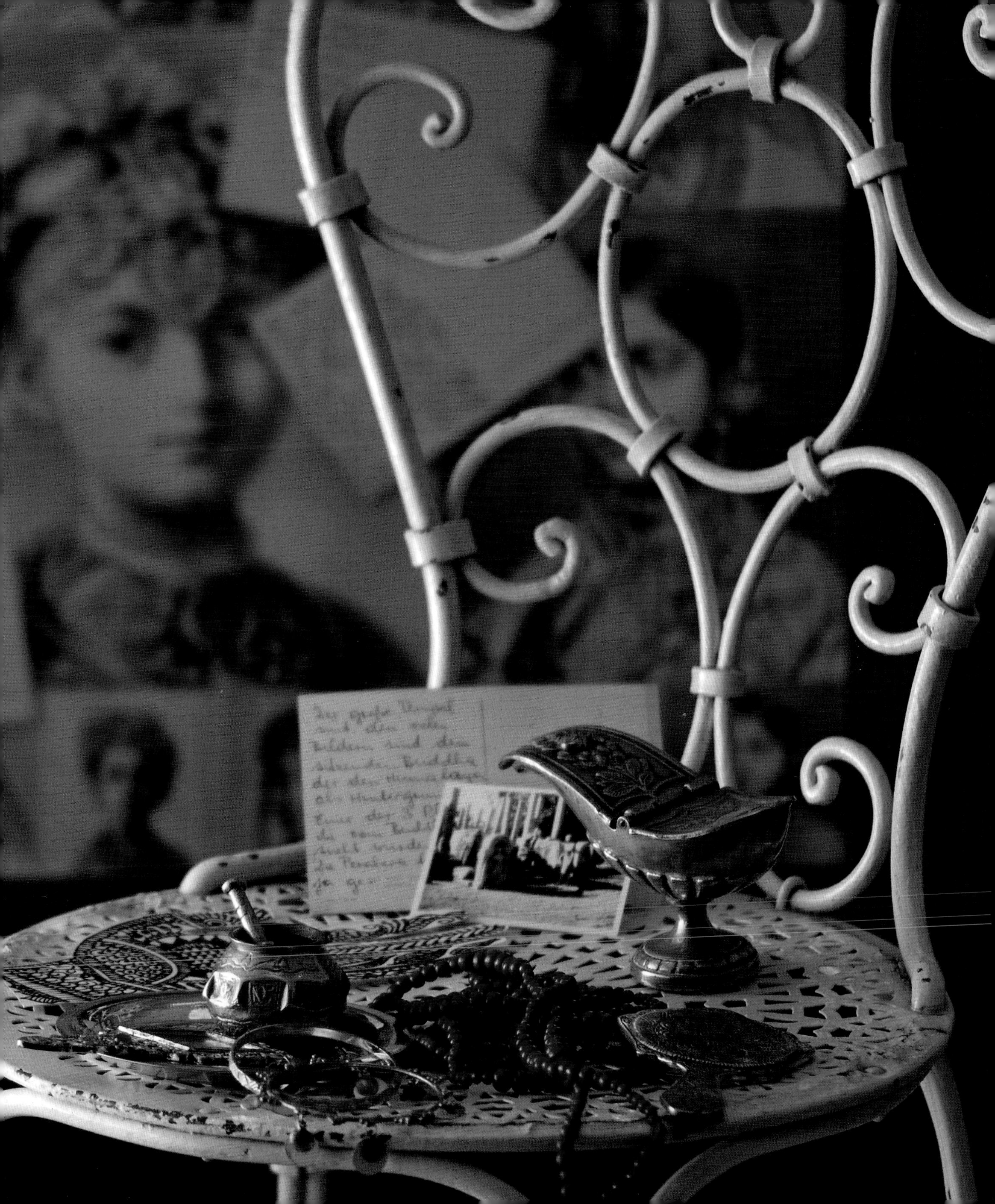

chapter one

Meet my family

I COULD NOT REALLY START THIS BOOK OF MEMORIES AND RECIPES WITHOUT MENTIONING MY SRI LANKAN ACHI (GRANDMOTHER), EMANONA WEERASEKERA KURUWITAGE. SHE WAS MARRIED TO MY SEYA (GRANDFATHER), ADRIAN SILVA KURUWITAGE, AND LIVED IN OUR ANCESTRAL HOME IN DEHIWALA, SRI LANKA. TO MY FATHER, SHE WAS A LOVING MOTHER AND THE RESPECTED UNOFFICIAL HEAD OF THE HOUSEHOLD. THE PEOPLE FROM THE VILLAGE ALL KNEW HER AS A WISE, GENEROUS PERSON WHO WOULD NOT PUT UP WITH ANYTHING THAT WAS NOT PROPER. TO ME SHE WAS A KIND, DOTING GRANDMOTHER WHO WAS ALWAYS THERE TO HAVE A CHAT AND OFFER ME FOOD. WE ENJOYED EACH OTHER'S COMPANY.

Achi was a walking encyclopaedia of Ayurvedic medicine and was always advising everyone on what or what not to eat when they were sick. I am still coming to grips with the heating and cooling properties of the various foods but they always played a very big part in the wellbeing and health of the household.

As I ponder my childhood years in Sri Lanka, I cannot remember one bad time. My world was full of love, respect and family. There were people everywhere and I was related to them all. To be a child in this household was bliss—people were always talking, laughing, joking and cooking, and although there were occasional disagreements it was a tight-knit unit of closely related people.

Perhaps I saw life through rose-coloured glasses because I was so young. And perhaps my memory is selective. But it's true that the adults in our household were very tolerant of my rascally escapades. The only times I feared Achi were when I cut or hurt myself—if she found out, some vile-tasting or very painful traditional Sri Lankan medicine would be brought out and liberally applied. As I was constantly scratching or cutting myself, Achi would frequently grab me when I whizzed by in my busy routine of playing in the fruit trees or in Dad's workshop, swiftly applying the dreaded lotion which was usually a concoction of special leaves, lime and an oil that stank. It would hurt like hell, but seemed to keep infections at bay.

I also have vivid memories of Mum chasing me around the gardens with a bottle of cod liver oil. By the time she caught me she was so angry that the stuff was forced down my throat—there were no capsules in those days, just a bottle of viscous disgusting oil.

One way or another, the women of our household managed to keep me relatively healthy despite our primitive surrounds.

According to the stories Achi told, Dad was a lot like me when he was a child, always running wild and getting into mischief. One of the stories involved Dad being ordered not to take the mangoes off the neighbour's tree. When he did and was caught, his father (my Seya) went to the market and bought a sack of mangoes, tied his son to a chair and forced him to eat the lot. Dad later recalled how Achi tried to compensate and, when he got into trouble from his father, how she would hide him in her room so he would not get a beating.

Times change, and with them, disciplinary styles. My Dad believed in tolerating childish naughtiness so long as it caused no real harm. He only ever hit me once, and I think that was out of pure frustration rather than anger. It was many years after we had left Sri Lanka to come to Australia. My younger brother David and I were always arguing about something and he had a habit of poking his tongue out at me. Eventually, after warning him for the hundredth time to stop, I punched him in the jaw and almost severed his tongue. Luckily, we were in Australia where decent emergency services and hospital care are available, and David and I were saved years of regret.

Our family compound in Dehiwala was more than 200 years old and contained two houses and a large engineering workshop. During my childhood years, it was home to six children and three sets of parents, as well as Achi and Seya. We kids played cricket in the courtyard, climbed the fruit trees and clambered through the bars of Achi's bedroom window en route to my auntie's house, where there always seemed to be a banana or special sweet treat waiting.

As Achi and Seya had four children, we were quite a clan.

My dad, Wickramapala Kuruvita, married my mum, Liselotte Katharina Fesel, an Austrian whom he met in London. Together they had three children: Philip Susantha Kuruvita, Peter Jayantha Kuruvita and David Sunjiva Kuruvita.

Auntie Nanda Kuruwitage married Stephen Gunatilleke and had one child: Mestiyage Dona Sarojini Visakha Gunatilleke.

Auntie Padmini Kusuma Kuruwitage was married to Kumarasena Ahangama and they had two children: Darashana Ahangama and Shakila Manori Ahangama.

Uncle Lionelapala was married to Violet and they had six daughters: Lasanda Sharmini (Chuti), Latana Sobani (Cubbie), Lilanjali Shashikala (Shashi), Lakmini Shriyangika (Lucky), Laianthika Subashini (Sita) and Lilani Saumya (Champa). (Uncle Lionel and his family lived nearby, but they were always at the compound; he was much younger than his siblings and spent a lot of time with Achi, particularly in her later years.)

These people were my universe.

We did not need anyone else—we did everything together. So it is not surprising that the structure of care in our Sri Lankan household was very strong. Achi nominated someone to look after each individual from the time they were born until the time they died. For example, Achi's youngest daughter Padmini was her carer; her housegirl and cook's assistant looked after Padmini's daughter, Manori; and as this woman got older Manori looked after her, right up until the time she passed away. To explain this to a Sri Lankan is not necessary as this is the norm, but for people not from our culture it may seem a bit foreign.

My mother cared for Seya (my grandfather) in his final few months. He was bedridden and covered in bedsores, and she bathed the wounds and stayed by his side right up to the moment of his death. My memories of this are a little vague but I do recollect people coming to remove any usable parts from his body and to embalm him. I was shown his corneas by the man who removed them—this was normal. It was explained that he was eighty-nine, had lived a good life and now he was dead. As simple as that. I accepted this, and life went on. To see dead people was as normal as seeing babies.

A funeral was a sad affair but the body of the loved one was kept in the house in an open coffin for three days beforehand, so everyone could come and pay their respects, and the soul had time to ensure that all was well and that those left behind had grieved and were ready to let go. Buddhist monks were invited in and chanted so the soul would be ready to leave the house and to be reborn into its next life cycle. If you had lived a good and pure life there was nothing to fear in death and the cycle would go on until you achieved Nirvana, after which you would not be reborn again.

But I remember the sense of extreme sorrow when Seya's coffin was lifted and taken outside the house to be carried to the funeral pyre for cremation. The women wailed and everyone cried—he was leaving his house for the last time. The family was so well respected that villagers lined the streets from our house all the way to the cemetery and had decorated the telegraph poles with white coconut blossoms; white is the colour of mourning in Buddhist culture. I held my Achi's hand for the entire five kilometre trek. It was the first time I ever saw my Dad cry.

After the funeral everyone came back to our house for an enormous feast which had been prepared with love and help from the ladies in the household. Other family members came from all over the country and brought the special foods of their regions.

It was part of our tradition to travel long distances to attend weddings and funerals as well as other important family gatherings.

When my Achi died, also at the age of eighty-nine, I was in Australia and was not there for the funeral. Fortunately, I had seen her the year before, and although she had lost her sight and was very frail we would sit together in the warm sunshine while she talked of old times and of how she missed her eldest son, my Dad.

In the
beginning

chapter two

In the beginning

SRI LANKA IS A COUNTRY RICH IN SPICES. WHILE ITS FORMALLY RECORDED HISTORY BEGAN OVER 2500 YEARS AGO, IT WAS IN THE SIXTEENTH CENTURY THAT CEYLON, AS IT WAS THEN KNOWN, WAS DISCOVERED BY THE PORTUGUESE. TRADE IN CINNAMON AND OTHER SPICES WAS SOON THRIVING. THE DUTCH AND BRITISH FOLLOWED, BRINGING WITH THEM THEIR OWN HISTORY AND INFLUENCES, AND ESTABLISHING A STRONG WESTERN PRESENCE IN THE ISLAND NATION.

Sri Lankan food is an expression of the country's rich history and is full of delightful surprises, just like the island itself. Characterised by vibrant colours and fragrant aromas, every dish, from main meals to desserts and cakes, makes use of the country's bounty of fresh spices. An ordinary Sinhalese curry, for example, can contain up to thirteen herbs and spices: chillies, coriander, cumin, curry leaves, fennel, fenugreek, garlic, ginger, lemongrass, lime, onion, pandanus leaf and turmeric.

It is no wonder, then, that spices are used by Sri Lankan people with such ease, not only creating food that is unique and interesting, but also accessing their healing properties as part of Ayurvedic medicine.

STOCKING THE SPICE RACK

I'll bet most of the spices in your cupboard are as old as your youngest child or sibling! But when it comes to spices, fresh is best. To revitalise your spice rack, why not go on an adventure and find the Sri Lankan spice store nearest you? And be sure to buy in small quantities: the fresher the spice, the better the flavour of your curry. Storage is important too: your spices should be stored in airtight jars away from direct light and heat.

Which ones to buy? With the following basics you will be ready to cook curry: cardamom, chillies (dried and fresh), cinnamon, cloves, coriander seeds, fenugreek, ginger, Goroka, fennel seeds, black mustard seeds, black peppercorns, cumin seeds, salt, tamarind, turmeric powder, curry powder, lemongrass, pandanus leaf.

It's a good idea to keep these other important ingredients on hand as well: Maldive fish flakes, ghee, coconut powder, onions and garlic.

If you are just beginning to use spices, try starting with a teaspoon of spice to a dish for four people, then add more according to taste. Remember that freshly ground spices release their flavours more readily. As spices enhance the natural flavour of your food you might also like to experiment by combining spices that complement each other to create new spice sensations.

Roasting of spices such as cumin, coriander and fennel seeds to bring out their flavour is a method used to make a black curry. The smell of a good curry powder being roasted can excite the senses to great heights!

RICE AND CURRY

Rice and curry form the staple diet of Sri Lankans who enjoy some of the spiciest foods in the world. Meat, poultry, fish and vegetables are prepared as curries while sliced onions, green chillies, black pepper, cinnamon, cardamom, cloves, nutmeg and saffron are used to add flavours.

A basic meal of rice and curry requires one fish (or beef or chicken) curry, two different vegetables, one portion of fried crispy stuff like poppadom, a malum (salad) of chopped leaves and coconut, and a hodda (gravy) of spices cooked with coconut milk.

The rice is always put on the plate first and curries are selected from the other dishes so you end up with a collection of minor meals around the plate. You eat with your hand, mixing the rice with some of the curry, forming the food into bite-sized balls and popping them into your mouth.

There is a vast range of flavours and different curry mixes used for different foods, and there are regional differences too. Even with the same base food, you can create completely different tastes. The way spices are combined and the quantities of each put a very personal signature onto a curry. You could eat the same kind of curry in a dozen homes in the same area, yet each will be slightly different.

Traditionally, there was no recipe book; knowledge was simply handed down to the daughters of the next generation. But modern life is diluting this process as people live and cook in separate kitchens, and pre-made spice mixes are now available.

CURRY POWDERS

In this section I will provide the basics for making great Sri Lankan curries, starting with the curry powders.

My grandmother used to make these curry powders into pastes by grinding them with a little water. She would have a row of colourful curry pastes in jars lined up along the top shelf of the cupboard so you could just combine all the other ingredients for a meal, then put a small amount of the paste into each dish to create the curry.

Here are some of our basic curry powder recipes.

Meat curry powder

Ingredients

4 long dried red chillies

25 g (1 oz/⅓ cup) coriander seeds

2 teaspoons fennel seeds

1 tablespoon cumin seeds

3 teaspoons fenugreek seeds

2 cloves

2 green cardamom pods, bruised

2 cm (¾ in) piece cinnamon stick

3 cm (1¼ in) piece pandanus leaf, optional

3 cm (1¼ in) piece lemongrass stem,
  bruised with the back of a knife

2 sprigs fresh curry leaves, leaves picked

½ teaspoon black mustard seeds

a pinch of ground turmeric

MAKES ABOUT 1 CUP

Method

Place all the ingredients except the turmeric in a heavy-based frying pan and dry roast over low heat for 7–10 minutes or until fragrant. Remove from the heat, stir in the turmeric and cool.

Using a spice grinder or mortar and pestle, grind the spices until a fine powder forms. Store in an airtight container, in a cool dark place, for up to 1 year.

Vegetable curry powder

This quick and easy-to-make curry powder is used to cook most Sri Lankan vegetable curries.

Ingredients

35 g (1¼ oz) coriander seeds	2 sprigs fresh curry leaves, optional,
2 tablespoons fennel seeds	leaves picked
2½ tablespoons cumin seeds	a large pinch of ground turmeric
1½ tablespoons fenugreek seeds	**MAKES ABOUT ¾ CUP**

Method

Place all the ingredients except the turmeric in a heavy-based frying pan and dry roast over low heat for 7–10 minutes or until fragrant. Remove from the heat, stir in the turmeric and cool.

Using a spice grinder or mortar and pestle, grind the spices until a fine powder forms. Store in an airtight container, in a cool dark place, for up to 1 year.

Roasted curry powder

Ingredients

35 g (1¼ oz) coriander seeds	4 fresh curry leaves
2 tablespoons cumin seeds	1 long dried red chilli (optional)
1 teaspoon fennel seeds	3 cm (1¼ in) piece dried pandanus leaf
2 cm (¾ in) piece cinnamon stick	1 teaspoon black peppercorns
5 cloves	2 teaspoons raw long-grain rice
¼ teaspoon green cardamom seeds	**MAKES ABOUT ½ CUP**

Method

Dry roast each ingredient separately in a small, heavy-based frying pan, shaking the pan continuously over low heat until fragrant (the coriander, cumin, fennel and rice must be fairly brown, but do not let them burn).

Cool and combine the spices, then, using a spice grinder or mortar and pestle, grind the mixture until a fine powder forms. Store in an airtight jar, in a cool dark place, for up to 2 months.

Fish curry powder

Ingredients

3 teaspoons black peppercorns

2 tablespoons cumin seeds

2 tablespoons fennel seeds

3 tablespoons coriander seeds

1½ teaspoons fenugreek seeds

2 cm (¾ in) piece lemongrass stem, bruised

1 sprig fresh curry leaves, leaves picked

MAKES ABOUT ¾ CUP

Method

Place all the ingredients in a heavy-based frying pan and dry roast over low heat for 7–10 minutes or until fragrant. Remove and reserve the curry leaves and lemongrass, then, using a spice grinder or mortar and pestle, grind the spices until a fine powder forms. Add the lemongrass and curry leaves and store in an airtight jar, in a cool dark place, for up to 2 months.

CHUTNEYS, SAMBALS AND PICKLES

No curry would be complete without being served with a condiment or two. There are so many, and they all have different qualities—some add heat, some are cooling and others add a little extra flavour. The following are my favourites.

Lime pickle

Tear off a little lime pickle and eat it with every mouthful of curry. Chopped lime pickle can also be combined with chopped fresh tomato, lime juice, Maldive fish flakes, onion and black pepper to make a fresh tomato and lime chutney.

Ingredients

20 limes	400 g (14 oz/ 1¾ cups) caster
250 g (9 oz) rock salt	(superfine) sugar
½ teaspoon black peppercorns	1 teaspoon dried chilli flakes
500 ml (17 fl oz/2 cups) white vinegar	**FILLS TWO 1 LITRE (35 FL OZ/4 CUPS) JARS**

Method

Using a sharp knife and working from the top to the bottom, cut the limes into quarters, making sure not to cut all the way through. Reserve any juices. Combine the salt and peppercorns, then stuff this into the limes and stand them upright on a tray.

Combine the remaining ingredients in a wide heavy-based saucepan, add any reserved juices and bring to the boil. Place the limes in the pan, cut side up, return to the boil, then cover and simmer over low heat for 10 minutes or until the limes turn yellow. Remove the pan from the heat and allow it to stand until cool.

Loosely layer the limes into two sterilised 1 litre (35 fl oz/4 cups) jars and pour the cooking liquid over them. Don't worry if the liquid does not cover the limes; this will happen in time. Seal and store in a cool dark place for at least 2 weeks before using.

Pol sambal

Fresh pol (coconut) sambal is great with everything and is served with nearly every meal, including breakfast, when it is eaten with egg hoppers and kiri bath.

When our houseboy Nehal brought us the crusty bread from the bakery next door it was still steaming hot. I used to love cutting thick slices of the bread and putting spoonfuls of pol sambal on it—it was delicious. The coconut oil would come out and the flavours would intensify.

When we first arrived in Australia in 1979 it was very hard to get a fresh coconut so we had to reconstitute desiccated coconut with some warm water. It is not as juicy as fresh coconut, but is an acceptable alternative.

I have used paprika solely to give the sambal a rich red colour; you can use more red chilli if you want it very hot.

Ingredients

1 teaspoon black peppercorns	1 large fresh coconut, scraped or 100 g
1 teaspoon Maldive fish flakes (see Glossary)	(3½ oz) desiccated coconut , combined
½ small red onion, finely chopped	with 100 ml (3½ fl oz) water
2 teaspoons chilli powder	juice of 1 lime
1 teaspoon hot paprika	**MAKES 2 CUPS**

Method

Place the peppercorns and Maldive fish flakes in a large mortar and grind with a pestle until a coarse paste forms. Add the onion, chilli powder and paprika and pound until a coarse paste forms, then add the coconut and pound until thoroughly combined. Stir in the lime juice, a little at a time so the sambal is not too sour, then season to taste with salt.

Sambal will keep, refrigerated, in an airtight container for up to 5 days.

Seeni sambal

This means 'sugar sambal' in Sinhalese, although the dish contains only a very small quantity of sugar. It is such an aromatic sambal it goes with everything, particularly meat, chicken or egg curries.

Ingredients

125 g (4½ oz) Maldive fish flakes (see Glossary)	3 cloves
80 g (2¾ oz) seedless tamarind pulp	1 cinnamon stick
125 ml (4 fl oz/½ cup) coconut milk (see Glossary)	3 cm (1¼ in) piece ginger, sliced
250 ml (9 fl oz/1 cup) vegetable oil	2 green cardamom pods, bruised
2 tablespoons coconut oil	5 cm (2 in) piece pandanus leaf
2 red onions, halved and thinly sliced	1 tablespoon caster (superfine) sugar
2 teaspoons chilli powder	2 teaspoons salt
1 sprig fresh curry leaves, leaves picked	juice of 1 lime
4 garlic cloves, crushed	**MAKES 2 CUPS**

Method

Pound the Maldive fish flakes in a mortar with a pestle until finely ground but not powdered. Combine the tamarind pulp and coconut milk in a bowl, then push through a fine sieve and discard any fibres.

Heat the oils in a heavy-based saucepan, add the onion, chilli powder, curry leaves, garlic, cloves, cinnamon, ginger, cardamom pods and pandanus leaf and cook over medium heat, stirring regularly, for 5 minutes or until onions are caramelised but not too dark. Stir in the remaining ingredients and cook for another 15 minutes or until the coconut milk is reduced and the onions are glossy.

Cool, then spoon into sterilised jars, seal and refrigerate. The sambal will harden upon refrigeration so will need to be warmed gently before serving.

Seeni sambal will keep, refrigerated, for 2–3 weeks.

Lunu miris

In Sinhalese 'salt chilli', this is the fiery one. It is extra hot and is finished with lime juice. Believe it or not, this condiment is used for breakfast foods such as milk rice and steamed cassava.

Once you start using it you won't be able to live without it.

Ingredients

25 g (1 oz/¼ cup) dried chilli flakes

8 black peppercorns

1 tablespoon Maldive fish flakes (see Glossary)

2 tablespoons finely chopped red onion

juice of 1 lime

MAKES ABOUT ⅓ CUP

Method

Place all the ingredients except the lime into a mortar and grind with a pestle until a paste forms. Stir in the lime juice and season to taste with salt.

Lunu miris will keep, refrigerated, for up to 3 days.

Mint sambal

This is more a South Indian accompaniment and is great with Dosai or Iddili. It is also delicious sprinkled on hot rice just before serving.

Ingredients

20 g (¾ oz/1 cup) (loosely packed) mint leaves, chopped

1 small red onion, finely chopped

5 cm (2 in) piece ginger, peeled and chopped

juice of ½ lime

3 long green chillies, halved, seeded and coarsely chopped

1 garlic clove, finely chopped

30 g (1 oz/⅓ cup) grated fresh coconut

MAKES ABOUT ½ CUP

Method

Place all the ingredients and ¼ cup water in a mortar and pestle or food processor and grind until smooth.

Mint sambal will keep, refrigerated, for up to 2 days.

Bringal pickle

Ingredients

1 kg (2 lb 4 oz) eggplant (aubergine), cut
   into 3 cm (1¼ in) pieces

5 long red chillies, cut into
   1 cm (½ in) pieces

1 small onion, cut into 1 cm (½ in) pieces

50 g (1¾ oz/½ cup) ground turmeric

vegetable oil, for deep-frying, plus 100 ml
   (3½ fl oz) extra

3 sprigs fresh curry leaves, leaves picked

1 tablespoon black mustard seeds

6 garlic cloves, finely chopped

200 g (7 oz) peeled ginger, finely chopped

60 g (2¼ oz/½ cup) ground cumin

125 g (4½ oz) caster (superfine) sugar

125 ml (4 fl oz/½ cup) white vinegar

2 teaspoons salt

MAKES 1 LITRE (35 FL OZ/4 CUPS)

Method

Place the eggplant, chillies and onion in a large bowl, add the ground turmeric and toss to coat well, then place in a large sieve and shake off the excess turmeric.

Fill a deep-fryer or large heavy-based saucepan one-third full of oil and heat to 180°C (350°F) or until a cube of bread dropped into the oil browns in 15 seconds. Working in small batches, cook the eggplant, chillies and onion until golden, then drain in a colander placed over a bowl and cool.

Heat the extra oil in a heavy-based saucepan, add the curry leaves and mustard seeds and cook over low heat just until the seeds start to pop. Add the garlic and ginger and cook for another 3 minutes, then add the cumin and cook for 2 minutes. Add the sugar, vinegar and salt and stir until the sugar dissolves and the mixture comes together.

Add the fried eggplant mixture to the pan and gently combine, trying not to break up the eggplant too much. Remove from the heat, cool, then spoon the pickle into a 1 litre (35 fl oz/4 cups) capacity sterilised jar, seal and refrigerate for at least 1 day before using.

The pickle will keep, refrigerated, for up to 1 month.

Tamarind chutney

This is a great accompaniment to a curry as it has a sweet and sour flavour and seems to bring the flavours together in your mouth. In Sri Lanka they also make it with dates and omit half the sugar; this gives the chutney a richer taste and adds texture.

My recipe is actually from a colleague I worked with on Vatulele Island in Fiji. Raymond Lee was the head chef of the resort on that island, previously owned by Australian producer and all-round nice guy Henry Crawford. My wife Karen and I had the pleasure of working there for two years. During that time I learned so much about cooking in the tropics, and my Sri Lankan buffet was always a treat.

Ray's method brought out all the fantastic flavours of the tamarind: the secret came right at the end of the process, adding fried mustard and curry leaves and covering it immediately so all the flavours stayed in the pot.

This chutney lasts and is actually easier to make in larger proportions.

When choosing your tamarind, get seedless and make sure the pulp is nice and soft, it should also be brown rather than black.

Ingredients

450 g (1 lb) tamarind pulp	650 g (1 lb 7 oz) raw sugar
150 g (5½ oz) ghee	1 teaspoon dried chilli flakes
1 onion, finely chopped	350 ml (12 fl oz) white vinegar
30 g (1 oz/¼ cup) finely chopped garlic	2 sprigs fresh curry leaves, leaves picked
30 g (1 oz/¼ cup) young ginger, finely chopped	2 tablespoons black mustard seeds
	MAKES 4 CUPS

Method

Soak the tamarind in 350 ml (12 fl oz) warm water for 5 minutes, then push through a fine sieve and discard any fibres.

Heat half the ghee in a heavy-based saucepan over low–medium heat and cook the onion, garlic and ginger for 3–5 minutes or until the onions are translucent.

Add the tamarind water, sugar, chilli flakes and vinegar and bring to the boil. Reduce the heat to low and cook, stirring regularly, for 1 hour or until the mixture has reduced by about three-quarters and is thick and pulpy.

Heat the remaining ghee in a small heavy-based frying pan over medium heat. Add the curry leaves and mustard seeds and shake the pan until the mustard seeds begin to pop, then immediately pour the seed mixture into the tamarind mixture, cover and cook for another 10 minutes. Remove the pan from the heat, transfer to a bowl and cool.

Season the chutney to taste with salt, then spoon it into two 500 ml (17 fl oz/2 cups) capacity sterilised jar and seal.

Tamarind chutney will keep for up to 1 year. Refrigerate after opening.

Acharu

Acharu is a spicy fruit salad. We used to enjoy this every Sunday at the polla or markets right outside our house. The flavours of green mango and guava with sweet ripe pineapple, plus chilli and vinegar, are outstanding.

Ingredients

50 g (1¾ oz) green mango, peeled and chopped

100 g (3½ oz) ripe pineapple, peeled and chopped

50 g (1¾ oz) green guava, peeled and chopped

1 small pawpaw, peeled and chopped

1 teaspoon chilli powder

1 teaspoon white vinegar

1 tablespoon caster (superfine) sugar

SERVES 4

Method

Place all the ingredients in a bowl, season to taste with salt and ground black pepper, then allow to stand for ½ hour so that the flavours mingle.

Eat with caution.

But beware: once you start you will not be able to stop!

COOKING RICE

Picking through rice was the first duty in our household. First thing in the morning after everyone was washed and the kids packed off to school the ladies of the house would sit in the cool morning sunlight and pick stones and other undesirable foreign matter out of the rice. Failure to do so could mean broken teeth and would leave you unable to enjoy your meal for fear of injury.

This job was compulsory; some say the white rocks were added to the rice on purpose to increase the weight of the sack. While this was true in some cases the contamination was mostly due to the primitive husking methods. In those days the rice was usually threshed on the side of the road and then pounded in large mortars with pestles to loosen the husks. I will always remember the rhythmic thud of the rice husking as three or four sets of people got going and it started to sound like music.

The other method I have seen, even on my last trip to Sri Lanka, is employed when the rice is for the farmer's own consumption. They simply put it onto the road and as the cars and trucks pass over it the husks are loosened. Once this is done they separate the rice from the husk by tossing it up into the air in a wicker basket open at one end. The lightweight husks are carried away by the wind and the rice falls back into the basket.

You can see that with either of these methods there are sure to be all types of foreign matter that need removing.

Dad was given a few acres of rice to farm from a friend of his, the Right Honourable General Sir John Lionel Kotelawala, CH, KBE, LLD, who was Prime Minister of Sri Lanka and Minister of Defence for several years in the 1950s. Erect and soldierly in his bearing, 'Sir John' as he was affectionately known was undoubtedly one of the most colourful personalities of his time. Always frank and outspoken, he never hesitated to call a spade a spade and always enjoyed a good story, even at his own expense. Anecdotes about his wit and rollicking sense of humour are told and retold to this day.

Beneath his tough exterior, Sir John was a kind-hearted and generous statesman who made numerous friends among a variety of people. Kandawala,

with its magnificent mansion and sprawling acres, was his home for well over five decades.

Being a soldier himself, he had a great regard for the military. In a final gesture of philanthropy and realising the need for a well-disciplined national security system, Sir John took the decision to bequeath his property to the nation for the establishment of a much-needed Defence Academy. The General Sir John Kotelawala Defence Academy is a fitting monument that stands as testimony to the character, patriotism and statesmanship of this great son of Sri Lanka.

I remember him as a kind old man who had an amazing estate that we would visit regularly, as our paddy fields were part of it. His house was like a museum— there were lion and tiger skins and all types of precious goods from all over the world. We were allowed to run free in the house and gardens—he even had his own zoo with an elephant that we would ride on and a gurami fish that he said was as old as he was.

Lunch was always a formal affair with all us kids getting a very stern talking to before we went in about how we were to behave. The table was so big that Sir John seemed to be a mile away. After lunch Dad and he would sit outside and talk while we explored his vast estate.

This gift of rice was a godsend to us when the years of Nationalisation started as there were food queues stretching for hundreds of metres. Luckily we lived next door to the village baker so bread was not a problem either.

Our houseboy Nehal would leave early in the morning to line up for necessities like sugar. I remember how Mum would give me and my brothers our sugar ration at the beginning of each month to do with as we pleased—but it had to last a month. I learned some very good budgeting lessons, and also how to care for things. If you didn't look after your sugar the ants would get in and then you would have to eat sugar with ants in it for a month.

The rice that Dad was in charge of was distributed equally throughout the estate, between the villagers who actually farmed it and Dad who managed it. It meant that we had enough to feed the whole family. My grandmother's day room was also the rice store and we would play on the large sacks whenever no one was looking.

Even though most people use rice cookers these days it is good to know a foolproof way of cooking rice without one.

I have found that if you measure your middle finger, for most adults the distance between the first joint and the end of the finger is relatively the same. This first joint is your own very portable water gauge.

Take the amount of raw rice you require and wash it thoroughly in cool water only once. Rice these days is so highly polished that if you wash it any more you will wash away any remaining goodness.

Now flatten the washed rice in the bottom of a large pot—the capacity should be at least ten times the volume of your rice—and add water until it reaches from the top of the rice to the first joint of your middle finger (for brown rice, add a little more).

Bring this to the boil uncovered and salted. Cook on a high heat until you can see the top of the rice and the water has evaporated to that level. Turn the stove's burner to its lowest setting and cover the pot with a tight-fitting lid. If you are using an electric cooker, have the hotplate next to the boiling pot on the lowest setting, and transfer the covered pot to it. Allow the rice to steam for about 10 minutes. Do not lift the lid or stir the rice—it will steam naturally and cook the rice so that it is fluffy and dry.

Once the rice is cooked remove the lid and, using the handle of a wooden spoon, fluff the rice and cover it again until you need it.

My grandmother's kitchen

chapter three
My grandmother's kitchen

MY ACHI'S KITCHEN WAS THE CENTRE OF OUR FAMILY'S UNIVERSE. IN IT, THERE WERE LOVE MATCHES, FIGHTS, DRUNKEN UNCLES, WEDDINGS, SPECIAL FULL MOON RITUALS, WONDERFUL FOOD AND THE TRAVELLING CHEFS WHO WOULD ARRIVE IN BULLOCK CARTS WITH THEIR MASSIVE POTS AND COOK FOR HUNDREDS. I FEEL VERY LUCKY TO HAVE BEEN GIVEN SOME OF THE RECIPES THAT WERE NURTURED THERE.

My childhood memories are flooded with recollections of the time, love and joy that went into the preparation of any meal from that kitchen. In fact, when I was quite young, Achi had a stool made for me so I could spend all my time in the kitchen with the women; I think that is how my understanding of passion for food was fostered.

There was no such thing as friends dropping over to this house—everyone was related in some way or another and it was considered very rude not to know how and to whom they were related.

These family members came from all parts of the country, bringing with them their regions' gourmet delicacies. All were greeted with great respect and everyone gathered around to hear their stories.

Piyadasa Kuruvitage, my uncle, was a tailor, and also a regular visitor to our house. He was known for his humour and for acting like the Yakka or devil. He was also famous for his unbelievable talent in knowing every one of our clan's addresses, so whenever there was a wedding, funeral or any special family gathering he would personally go to everyone's house, arriving with the traditional method of invitation—a wad of betel leaves. When this man died so did his knowledge of all the families' addresses. Believe it or not, no one had ever bothered to write them down, so it was very hard to gather everyone to his funeral.

When he came to visit, we would turn off all the lights and he would go into my grandmother's room and start making eerie noises behind the curtain before bursting out with a flashlight in his mouth and doing a crazy dance. This scared the wits out of all the children, but everyone laughed.

At Achi's we would always be entertained by someone, and the constant conversations were as normal then as the background noise of a TV is today; I much prefer the old ways.

Although Achi was in total control of the kitchen her two daughters were the faithful apprentices. A deaf and mute lady, Premawathi Prera, who had been adopted by the family, was the hard-working 'gofer' who picked, chopped, sorted and sieved all the ingredients so that one of my aunties could cook them under the watchful eye of Achi. A perfectionist and the feared master cook, Achi was given to occasionally throwing things and screaming at her daughters. As both my aunties will attest, she would taste absolutely everything to ensure the seasoning was correct.

The amount of salt and sugar needed in a dish would be discussed for a while before being added. Even then, Achi would probably come along and pop in one more pinch of sugar or a little bit more salt or lime.

There was a lot of pressure in Achi's kitchen. The celebrity chefs of today have nothing on my grandmother in full flight. Her food was delectable and remains the cornerstone for my style of Sri Lankan cooking. Achi's daughters have taught their daughters who are now in control but still being watched and guided by my aunties.

Kiri hoddy

When we arrived from England I was thoroughly British, cockney accent and all. Although Dad always cooked curry in the UK, I don't think we ate it much. When every meal in our new home involved spicy food we all had to be eased into it.

I soon earned the name kiri hodda (milk gravy boy)—kiri hoddy is the beginner's curry, more or less the béchamel sauce of Sri Lankan cookery.

You can have it plain; but it's also great with many vegetables and tastes uniquely Sri Lankan.

Ingredients

1 onion, thinly sliced

1 small green chilli, halved lengthways

4–6 fresh curry leaves

2 cm (¾ in) piece pandanus leaf

2 garlic cloves, thinly sliced

½ teaspoon ground turmeric

½ teaspoon fenugreek seeds

1 teaspoon Maldive fish flakes (see Glossary) (optional)

500 ml (17 fl oz/2 cups) coconut cream (see Glossary)

1 tablespoon lime juice

SERVES 6

Method

Put all the ingredients except the coconut cream and lime juice into a heavy-based saucepan, add 1 cup of water and simmer over low heat for 10 minutes or until the onions are soft. Stirring continuously, add the coconut cream and stir for a further 1–2 minutes. Do not let the mixture boil. Remove from the heat, season to taste with salt and add the lime juice.

Note: It is important to keep stirring the mixture after adding the coconut cream to prevent the kiri hoddy from coagulating.

LIFE AT HOME

Part of our compound was a huge factory my Dad built soon after we arrived from London. There was plenty going on and I have many memories from this time, but one in particular that none of us will ever forget.

When my younger brother David, also known as Gunga, was little, he was carried everywhere; as the only one born in Sri Lanka he was a definite favourite with my aunties and our Achi. One day, though, he was left unattended and, seeing that the workers on the lathes in the workshop had run out of water, he decided to take their glass water bottle and fill it up—he had seen them do this a hundred times before. He managed to make it up the steep bathroom steps but fell on the way down, landing on the bottle and gashing his chest very deeply in about five places. This caused pandemonium, the women screaming and Mum and Dad rushing to get him to hospital wrapped in a blood-soaked towel. He survived but still has the jagged scar to attest to his and Mum's trauma.

Despite occasional dramas of this kind, we kids generally had a fun and easy life. Mum was settling into the Sri Lankan way of doing things and Dad worked hard to support us all.

THE POLLA

The polla, or market, across the road had everything and it went late into the night, right outside our family compound. The food came from all over the area and was always fresh. Dad and my aunties were great hagglers, so it was often very exciting. I loved the polla—we spent hours walking around learning about the produce. I also learned the seasons and yearned for the exotics like jakfruit and mangosteen and rambutan to arrive. Jakfruit are large spiky fruits which grow on the trunks of massive trees. When you peel them they ooze a sticky gum—the stallholders would rub palm oil on their hands to soften it and then, using a piece of paper, rub it off. The fruit was then shredded and placed in a pile so the cooks of the different houses could take it home for malum (salad).

As well as fresh produce, the polla sold cooked food from stalls. People in small tin sheds fried masalawadde, a Tamil lentil patty which is delicious with a beer, and

is also a favourite travelling food. Every town and city you travel through will have someone frying fresh wadde on the side of the road. I still remember the clanging of the griddle as kottu rotti was chopped with two steel choppers. This noise was with us every day, sometimes till three in the morning, and my Dad made frequent trips across the road to ask them politely to keep it down. Having the annoying noise did not mean that we weren't customers, though. The food was good and piping hot around the clock. It was something my Dad would chase for the rest of his life: 'the taste'. I feel very lucky to have been given some of these recipes and 'the taste' is something that I too continually strive to achieve.

All of the cooking at these stalls was done by wood fire. Kerosene was a luxury and it was only just before we left for Australia in 1974 that they got fuel stoves.

We also had a butcher across the road who would have a carcass of beef hanging up in his open thatched coconut-leaf shed. There were no particular cuts of beef—you would just ask for a good piece. Brushing the flies away, the butcher would sharpen his home-made hatchet on a stone and cut us a piece from the ribs or rump, then wrap it in a giant leaf my Mum called elephant ears.

There was a certain rich businessman who was big in the spice trade. He was neurotic about being killed or robbed and was always heavily armed. This man would get out of his car, walk up to the butcher and show the 45 Magnum hanging from his waist. I'm sure he always got the best bit of beef.

The butcher's son taught me how to speak Sinhalese; we played cars in the dust in my Dad's workshop across the road. Mum said I was fluent in one month. Not bad—from a cockney lad to a Sri Lankan in thirty days.

The polla today has grown with the town and now stretches further than I remember. It is packed with all the freshest fruit, vegetables, freshly killed pork and a vast variety of fish. People bring the produce from Petal market in town and off the farms in the interior. When you purchase fish or meat the stallholders clean and chop it for you using massive crescent-shaped knives which have been sharpened on stone or on the roof guttering.

My first cousin and his son have a stall from which my auntie still buys all her vegetables.

MEAT CURRIES

The main meat market near our compound was at the end of Hill Street in Dehiwala Junction. It was a seven-day-a-week operation and was run by the Muslim community. I was always the first to put my hand up when someone was going—it was so exciting and colourful. (The market is still there, with the sons of the original butchers now running the show.)

Getting dressed up was a must—it is wonderful to live in a country where people, no matter how poor they are, will always ensure they are well turned out before leaving the house. I had to put pomade in my hair and comb it, ensure I had on a collared shirt and long trousers, and put something on my feet. Formal shoes were optional but some kind of footwear was essential.

Once ready, smelling and looking like a peach, I would head out with my aunties, all of them wearing saris, and walk down to the Junction.

One thing you realise when you go to a butcher in a developing country is that currying or stewing the meat is essential, and not a choice. Firstly, the meat is not aged. The beast hanging in the open shop outside a major bus stop was probably having breakfast that very same morning. This means the meat is always very tough. The other reason to cook a curry for a long while is that there is no refrigeration; if you buy meat in the afternoon you need to cook the hell out of it to make sure it is sterilised. Have you ever wondered why people fresh out of Asia think you are mad for having a steak with blood in it? To them, it would seem like playing Russian roulette with your stomach.

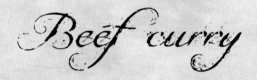

Beef curry

There are a number of Sri Lankan recipes for beef curry. Some have coriander leaves, others are fenugreek based. But I want to give you the house beef curry from our ancestral home in Dehiwala. My Dad modified it further when we were in Australia by adding a tablespoonful of tomato paste to enhance the richness.

    This curry is not meant to be mild. It should be fiery and bring out beads of perspiration on your forehead while you are eating it. The flavours will really mingle if the curry is made in the morning and consumed for your evening meal.

Ingredients

450 g (1 lb) topside or chuck steak, cut into 2 cm (¾ in) pieces

1 teaspoon ground cumin

1½ teaspoons chilli powder

1 teaspoon ground coriander

4 cloves

2 teaspoons Sri Lankan meat curry powder (see page 30)

½ teaspoon fenugreek seeds, lightly roasted

2 green cardamom pods, bruised

1 cinnamon stick

½ teaspoon ground turmeric

½ teaspoon Sri Lankan roasted curry powder (see page 36)

½ teaspoon salt

½ teaspoon freshly ground black pepper

5 cm (2 in) piece pandanus leaf

2 cm (¾ in) piece ginger, peeled and thinly sliced

2 tablespoons vegetable oil

1 small onion, finely chopped

2 garlic cloves, finely sliced

1 sprig fresh curry leaves, leaves picked

1 tablespoon tomato paste (concentrated purée) (optional)

1 beef stock cube (bouillon) (optional)

SERVES 6

Method

Place the meat, spices, pandanus leaf and ginger in a large bowl and toss to combine well.

Heat the oil in a large heavy-based saucepan over low heat, add the onion, garlic and curry leaves and cook for 3–5 minutes or until the onions are soft but not brown. Increase the heat to high, then add the meat and stir for 3–4 minutes or until the meat is evenly coloured. Cover with 1 litre (35 fl oz/4 cups) of water, then add the tomato paste and stock cube. Bring to the boil, then reduce the heat to low and simmer for 45 minutes or until the beef is tender and the sauce is thick.

Chicken curry

Choosing a chicken is a fine art, and there are two types: a curry chicken and a broiler. We always shopped for the curry chicken.

The curry chicken stall was in the corner of the polla and it had two rooms—one contained twenty or so live cowering white chickens, and the other was lined with a thick black sheet of plastic. This was the slaughterhouse.

The butchers were jolly guys who would always be smiling and joking. They wore blood-splattered sarongs and singlets. As with the beef, there was no refrigeration so the poultry was slaughtered to order. The chickens were always sold skinless as it was a lot quicker for the men to rip the feathers off with the skin rather than to pluck them.

The meat was cut up for us and placed in a large 'elephant ears' leaf. When we got home all we had to do was add the spices and cook the curry.

Ingredients

THICKENING MIXTURE

1 tablespoon raw long-grain rice

1 tablespoon grated fresh or
  desiccated coconut

2 small green chillies, halved lengthways

3 green cardamom pods

2 cloves

CURRY

1 size 14 chicken (1.4 kg/3 lb 2 oz), cut into
  14 pieces

2 teaspoons ground cumin

2 tablespoons ground coriander

2 teaspoons chilli powder

½ teaspoon ground turmeric

½ teaspoon fenugreek seeds, lightly roasted

2 teaspoons Sri Lankan meat curry
  powder (see page 30)

½ cinnamon stick

½ teaspoon black mustard seeds

1 teaspoon salt

100 ml (3½ fl oz) vegetable oil

1 onion, finely chopped

2 garlic cloves, thinly sliced

5 cm piece (2 in) pandanus leaf

1 sprig fresh curry leaves, leaves picked

SERVES 6

Method

To make the thickening mixture, place the rice and coconut in a small heavy-based frying pan and shake over low heat for 3–4 minutes or until the coconut is nut brown. Place the rice and coconut into a mortar with the rest of the thickening mixture ingredients and 2 tablespoons of water and pound with a pestle until a fine paste forms.

Place the chicken pieces in a large bowl, add all the spices except for the mustard seeds and salt and toss to coat well. Add the thickening mixture and combine well.

Heat the oil in a large heavy-based saucepan over medium heat, add the onion, garlic, pandanus leaf, curry leaves and mustard seeds and cook until the mustard seeds begin to pop. Add the chicken and stir until well coated, then add the salt and 1 litre (35 fl oz/4 cups) of water and scrape the bottom of the pan with a wooden spoon to remove any cooked pieces. Bring to the boil, then reduce the heat to low and simmer gently for 20 minutes or until the chicken is tender.

FISH AND SEAFOOD CURRIES

When making a fish curry always search for a firm-fleshed fish. Tuna, mackerel and large trevally work really well. There are many different fish curries, but I will start by giving you some of my favourite recipes.

A white curry is highly spiced but not too hot, while the black miris malu or chilli fish will cause more than your brow to sweat. Ambul thial, a dry curry, is fantastic when you're travelling; it was always one of the favourites when we made lunch packets.

The variations are huge; which one you choose depends on the size of the fish, where it is from (fresh or salt water) and who is eating it. There is even a separate method for cooking the head of big and juicy reef fish.

Some recipes ask for tomatoes, but I have never added tomatoes to a fish curry and they were never used in my grandmother's house either.

White curry

Ingredients

juice of 2 limes

450 g (1 lb) Spanish mackerel, skin on, cut into 3 cm (1¼ in) pieces

1 piece Goroka (see Glossary)

300 ml (7 fl oz) coconut milk (see Glossary)

2 teaspoons Sri Lankan fish curry powder (see page 39)

½ cinnamon stick

½ teaspoon ground turmeric

½ teaspoon fenugreek seeds, lightly roasted

½ teaspoon dill seeds

1 onion, finely chopped

3 small green chillies, halved lengthways

2 garlic cloves, thinly sliced

1 sprig fresh curry leaves, leaves picked

100 ml (3½ fl oz) coconut cream (see Glossary)

SERVES 6

Method

Place half the lime juice and 60 ml (2 fl oz/¼ cup) of cold water in a shallow bowl, add the mackerel and gently wash the fish all over. Drain the liquid, then add the Goroka and allow to stand for 10 minutes.

Place the coconut milk, spices, onion, chillies, garlic and curry leaves in a heavy-based saucepan, bring to the boil and simmer for 10 minutes or until the onions are soft. Add the drained fish and Goroka and simmer gently for 5–7 minutes or until the fish is nearly cooked through. Add the coconut cream and bring to just below the boil, being careful not to let the mixture boil. Remove from the heat, cover and stand for 10 minutes, then season to taste with salt and the remaining lime juice if needed.

Miris malu

Also known as chilli fish, this curry is best when eaten with freshly grated coconut and freshly boiled cassava.

Ingredients

2 trevally, about 200–300 g (7–10½ oz) each, cleaned	3 garlic cloves, thinly sliced
1 tablespoon chilli powder	2 pieces Goroka (see Glossary)
2 teaspoons freshly ground black pepper	2 cm (¾ in) slice ginger
1 teaspoon ground cumin	1 onion, thinly sliced
2 teaspoons ground coriander	1 sprig fresh curry leaves, leaves picked
4 green cardamom pods, bruised	5 cm (2 in) piece pandanus leaf
1 cinnamon stick	1 small green chilli, halved lengthways
1 teaspoon fenugreek seeds, lightly roasted	**SERVES 6**

Method

Using a cleaver or large knife, chop each fish into 6 pieces and, if using the heads, split each in half.

Place all the spices except for the fenugreek seeds in a heavy-based frying pan and dry roast over low heat for 7–10 minutes or until fragrant.

Place the garlic, Goroka, fenugreek seeds, ginger and roasted spices in a mortar and grind with a pestle until a fine paste forms.

Place the fish, spice paste and remaining ingredients in a heavy-based saucepan. Add 1 litre (35 fl oz/4 cups) cold water, bring to the boil and simmer gently for 10 minutes or until the fish is just cooked through, then remove from the heat and season to taste with salt.

Ambul thial

This is a favourite in Sri Lanka—there are many recipes for this dry fish curry, but its signature flavours are Goroka, black pepper, chilli and lime. My recipe is more complex than many and has been pulled straight out of our family kitchen.

Traditionally, Ambul thial is cooked in an earthenware chatty (clay pot) stacked between two other chatties filled with hot coals so that the food is cooked from above and below and tastes slightly smoky.

In a modern kitchen, you might need to resort to cooking Ambul thial in the oven.

Ingredients

450 g (1 lb) tuna steak, cut into 3 cm (1¼ in) pieces

juice of 1 lime

5 pieces Goroka (see Glossary), soaked in tepid water for 30 minutes

6 garlic cloves, crushed

2 cm (¾ in) piece ginger, peeled and coarsely chopped

1 tablespoon chilli powder

½ teaspoon ground cumin

1 teaspoon ground coriander

½ teaspoon Sri Lankan roasted curry powder (see page 36)

2 green cardamom pods, seeded

2 teaspoons freshly ground black pepper

1 teaspoon salt

1 cinnamon stick

2 sprigs fresh curry leaves, leaves picked

2 small green chillies, halved lengthways

SERVES 6

Method

Combine the tuna and lime juice in a bowl, drain, then place the tuna in a single layer in a large heavy-based saucepan. Drain the Goroka, place in a mortar with the garlic, ginger and all the spices except the cinnamon and and pound with a pestle until a paste forms. Combine the paste with 250 ml (9 fl oz/1 cup) of water, then add the cinnamon, curry leaves and chillies. Pour this over the fish and combine well.

Cook the fish over low–medium heat until it comes to the boil, then simmer gently for 5 minutes or until most of the liquid has evaporated.

Sprats white curry

Sprats are usually anchovies and can be bought either fresh or dried. They are also called ha imasso or rice flies.

I will give two of my favourite sprats recipes. The white curry recipe uses dried sprats and coconut cream, which really brings out the flavour of the fish and also softens them. The second recipe is for a classic fresh sprat curry.

When shopping for dried fish of any kind, only buy those with no heads (the intestines should also come out when the heads are removed). Make sure there is not a lot of fine dust in the packet as dust indicates that the fish are old. Always wash dry fish to remove any impurities, then pat them dry again.

When using fresh sprats, remove the heads and intestines in one move, then wash the fish in water, salt and Goroka.

Ingredients

200 g (7 oz) headless dried sprats	¼ teaspoon dill seeds
1 small onion, finely chopped	½ teaspoon chilli powder
2 small green chillies, chopped	200 ml (7 fl oz) coconut milk (see
1 teaspoon fenugreek seeds, lightly	Glossary)
roasted	juice of ½ a lime
1 sprig fresh curry leaves, leaves picked	100 ml (3½ fl oz) coconut cream
2 garlic cloves, thinly sliced	(see Glossary)
½ teaspoon ground turmeric	SERVES 6

Method

Wash the sprats well and place them in a saucepan with all the ingredients except the lime juice and the coconut cream. Bring to the boil.

Reduce the heat to low, cover and simmer for 5 minutes, then add the lime juice and coconut creams. Stir continuously for a further 2 minutes to stop the curry from curdling. Remove from the heat and season to taste.

Fresh sprats curry

Ingredients

250 g (9 oz) fresh sprats (anchovies or
    large whitebait), heads discarded, cleaned

2 pieces Goroka (see Glossary), smashed

1 teaspoon ground turmeric

2 teaspoons chilli powder

100 ml (3½ fl oz) vegetable oil

¼ teaspoon dill seeds

2 onions, finely chopped

3 long dried red chillies, broken

2 sprigs fresh curry leaves, leaves picked

juice of ½ a lime

½ teaspoon caster (superfine) sugar

SERVES 6

Method

Rinse the fish in cold water, then place in a heavy-based saucepan. Dissolve 1 teaspoon
of salt in 150 ml (5 fl oz) water, then pour this over the fish. Add the Goroka, turmeric and
chilli powder and simmer over medium heat until the water has evaporated.

Carefully remove the fish from the pan, trying not to break them up and place in
a bowl. Wipe the pan clean, then heat the oil over low heat and cook the dill seeds, onion,
chillies and curry leaves for 3 minutes. Gently stir in the fish, then, stirring continuously,
add the lime juice and sugar, season to taste with salt, and remove from the heat.

Squid curry

Ingredients

350 g (12 oz) medium squid, cleaned, heads and tentacles reserved

3 pieces Goroka (see Glossary)

¼ teaspoon fennel seeds

½ teaspoon chilli powder

½ teaspoon ground turmeric

1 teaspoon ground cumin

1½ teaspoons ground coriander

¼ teaspoon fenugreek seeds

½ teaspoon finely ground black pepper

50 g (1¾ oz) ghee

½ onion, finely chopped

3 garlic cloves, thinly sliced

1 sprig fresh curry leaves, leaves picked

2 small green chillies, chopped

300 ml (10½ fl oz) coconut milk (see Glossary)

100 ml (3½ fl oz) coconut cream (see Glossary)

juice of ½ lime

SERVES 6

Method

Cut the squid tubes into 1 cm (½ in) thick slices, then place in a bowl with the tentacles, cleaned heads, Goroka and all the spices and combine well.

Heat the ghee in a heavy-based saucepan over medium heat, add the onion, garlic, curry leaves and chilli and cook, stirring frequently for 4 minutes or until golden. Increase the heat to high, add the squid and stir for 3 minutes, then add the coconut milk, reduce the heat to low and simmer for 10 minutes or until the squid is tender. Stir in the coconut cream and lime juice and season to taste with salt. You should be left with a thick dark sauce.

VEGETARIAN CURRIES

Vegetarian curries as well as a malum (salad) are included with almost every meal in Sri Lanka. As my Achi was a vegetarian, I had no trouble finding a good selection of recipes straight from her kitchen.

Malum

A malum is a cooked salad which usually consists of green leafy vegetables or herbs plus anything from banana blossom to green jakfruit.

Ingredients

1 bunch flat-leaf (Italian) parsley, leaves picked and finely chopped

½ small onion, finely chopped

1 small green chilli, finely chopped

50 g (1¾ oz) freshly grated coconut

½ teaspoon ground Maldive fish flakes (see Glossary)

¼ teaspoon ground turmeric

juice of ½ lime

SERVES 6

Method

Place all the ingredients except the lime juice in a saucepan and stir over medium heat for 4 minutes or until just warm. It is important to keep the bright green colour in the leafy ingredients.

Remove from the heat, stir in the lime juice and season to taste with salt.

Breadfruit curry

Breadfruit is such a versatile fruit. Grown on a tree about 7 metres tall with beautiful fan-like leaves, this delicately flavoured fruit has to be picked at exactly the right time. When choosing a breadfruit, make sure the skin is not too green and is unmarked but also that it is not too soft. It should be a dull green and sometimes it even has a mottled look.

Coming from the tropics it is seasonal; your greengrocer should be able to advise you about availability. Don't bother with the tinned variety as the flavour and texture has been taken away in the canning process.

In Fiji and all over Asia breadfruit is made into chips and served with various dips, or just seasoned with salt and chilli. The Fijians also boil it and use it as the starch content of their meal. If you decide to try this, strain the breadfruit thoroughly once it's cooked, then leave it covered for a few minutes. The result is that the breadfruit fluffs up and is beautiful to eat.

This curry is a favourite at home in Sri Lanka; my Auntie Padmini always has one waiting when we go to visit.

Ingredients

CURRY

1 teaspoon ground coriander

1 teaspoon ground cumin

1 teaspoon vegetable curry powder
(see page 33)

1 breadfruit, about 500 g (1 lb 2 oz),
peeled and cut into 3 cm (1¼ in) pieces

2 small green chillies, halved lengthways

1 small onion, finely chopped

1 sprig fresh curry leaves, leaves picked

½ teaspoon ground turmeric

½ teaspoon freshly ground black pepper

3 cm (1¼ in) piece cinnamon stick

300 ml (10½ fl oz) coconut milk (see Glossary)

100 ml (3½ fl oz) coconut cream (see Glossary)

a pinch of roasted curry powder
(see page 36)

FOR TEMPERING

50 ml oil

1 small onion, chopped

5 cm piece pandanus leaf

2 cloves garlic

1 teaspoon mustard seeds

1 sprig curry leaves

SERVES 6

Method

For the curry, place the coriander, cumin and vegetable curry powder in a small heavy-based frying pan and dry roast over low heat until dark brown.

Place the roasted spices and all the ingredients except the coconut cream and roasted curry powder in a heavy-based saucepan and simmer for 12 minutes or until the breadfruit is tender.

Stirring continuously, add the coconut cream and cook for another 4 minutes or until just below the boil. Do not boil. The sauce should be thick and the breadfruit soft and tender. Season to taste with salt, sprinkle with the roasted curry powder and serve. Do not stir in the roasted curry powder.

To temper, heat the oil and fry the onion, pandanus leaf, garlic and mustard seeds until light brown. Add the curry leaves and pour over the cooked curry.

Green mango curry

We had a massive mango tree in the courtyard linking all the houses in our family compound. My Achi told me it had been there for as long as she could remember. At a guess, it would have been over 120 years old. It stood about 15 metres tall and was wide enough at the base for us to play chasings around it.

During Vesak, which is the festival that celebrates the birth, death and enlightenment of Lord Buddha, the country comes alight with homemade lanterns. We used to build a massive and elaborate lantern which Nehal, our houseboy, would take to the very top of the tree and light. It always looked so beautiful. One year we all came out to admire our creation. As we watched, a large gust of wind knocked over the candle in the lantern and the months of work went up in a massive ball of flame. We all thought it was great—it could be seen for kilometres.

Unfortunately, the tree had to be cut down when the road was widened fifteen or so years ago. The fruit were huge teardrop-shaped mangoes which were absolutely fantastic to eat, whether you had them green in an acharu (pickle) or ripe from the tree. We had so many that green mango curry was a weekly feature during the season.

This is an unusual curry that has a bit of a sweet and sour flavour with a good jolt of chilli. Texturally it is great, as you include the stone which is similar to having a bone in a meat curry. The flavours get trapped in the stone and fibre, and when eating with your fingers you really get to suck the flavour out of it.

Please note that this recipe calls for mature mango—this means the skin is green but the flesh has started to turn yellow.

Some green mango curry recipes call for ground mustard seed; I feel this is unnecessary, but try it both ways.

Ingredients

450 g (1 lb) green mangoes

1 tablespoon salt

1 teaspoon ground cumin

1 teaspoon ground coriander

2 cm (¾ in) piece cinnamon stick

50 g (1¾ oz) ghee

1 onion, finely chopped

1 sprig fresh curry leaves, leaves picked

3 cm (1¼ in) piece pandanus leaf

2 cm (¾ in) piece lemongrass, bruised

3 small green chillies, chopped

3 cm (1¼ in) piece ginger, peeled and chopped

½ teaspoon dried chilli flakes

1 tablespoon caster (superfine) sugar

1 tablespoon malt vinegar

1 teaspoon Maldive fish flakes (see Glossary), coarsely pounded

¼ teaspoon ground turmeric

400 ml (14 fl oz) coconut milk (see Glossary)

SERVES 6

Method

Wash, peel and cut each mango through the stone into 8 pieces, then toss in a bowl with the salt, cover with cold water and stand for 30 minutes. Drain the mango pieces and rinse well.

Place the cumin, coriander and cinnamon in a small heavy-based frying pan and roast over low heat until fragrant, then set aside.

Heat the ghee in a heavy-based saucepan over medium heat, add the onion, curry leaves, pandanus leaf, lemongrass, green chilli and ginger and cook for 5 minutes or until the onion is soft. Add the mangoes, chilli flakes, sugar and vinegar and cook for another 5 minutes, then stir in the Maldive fish flakes, turmeric, coconut milk and the roasted spices. Simmer for 15 minutes or until the mango is tender and the sauce has thickened. Remove from the heat and season to taste with salt.

Snake bean curry

This is such a tasty curry and as far as I am concerned, the best way to deal with the unusual flavour that a snake (yard-long) bean has.

When selecting snake beans, choose ones that are nice and stiff with the seeds tightly held in the skin. You should also look for a lovely purple tip on the ends of the beans.

Ingredients

350 g (12 oz) snake (yard-long) beans, washed and cut into 5 cm (2 in) lengths

2 small green chillies, chopped

1 teaspoon dried chilli flakes

1 onion, finely chopped

1 sprig fresh curry leaves, leaves picked

¼ teaspoon ground turmeric

1 teaspoon ground cumin

½ teaspoon fenugreek seeds

½ teaspoon fennel seeds

2½ tablespoons vegetable oil

125 ml (4 fl oz/½ cup) coconut cream (see Glossary)

SERVES 6

Method

Toss the beans in a bowl with all the ingredients except the oil and coconut cream.

Heat the oil in a heavy-based frying pan over high heat until the oil just begins to smoke. Add the bean mixture and stir for 5 minutes, then add the coconut cream, reduce the heat to low and simmer until the cream has reduced by half. Remove from the heat and season to taste with salt.

Cashew nut curry

The cashew nut is amazing. It comes from one of very few plants where the seed grows outside the fruit. When ripe the cashew apple is an exotic-flavoured delicate little bell. Connected to the bottom of this red or yellow bell is the cashew nut, wrapped in a skin and protected by caustic oil that can burn your fingers.

The cleaning process is time-consuming and potentially painful because of the caustic oil. Luckily, we can buy raw cashews and save our fingers.

Ingredients

250 g (9 oz) raw cashew nuts

300 ml (10½ fl oz) coconut milk (see Glossary)

1 teaspoon chilli powder

1 teaspoon cumin seeds, dry roasted and ground

½ teaspoon ground turmeric

1 tablespoon Maldive fish flakes (see Glossary), ground

3 small green chillies, finely chopped

3 cm (1¼ in) piece pandanus leaf

2 cm (¾ in) piece cinnamon stick

50 g (1¾ oz) ghee

2 onions, finely chopped

1 sprig fresh curry leaves, leaves picked

½ teaspoon dill seeds

a pinch of roasted curry powder (see page 36)

SERVES 6

Method

Cover the cashews with cold water and soak them for 30 minutes, then drain.

Place the cashews, coconut milk, chilli powder, cumin, turmeric, Maldive fish flakes, green chilli, pandanus leaf and cinnamon stick in a heavy-based saucepan, bring to the boil and simmer for 10 minutes or until the cashews are tender, then remove from the heat.

Heat the ghee in a frying pan, add the onion, curry leaves and dill seeds and cook over medium heat for 4 minutes or until the onions are golden. Pour in the cashew curry mixture and cook for another 5 minutes. Season to taste with salt, sprinkle with a little roasted curry powder and serve. Do not stir in the curry powder.

Curried ladies fingers

These little green ladies fingers (okra) are so tasty but unfortunately the sliminess of them puts some people off. In this recipe they are fried first and then curried. This helps to reduce the sliminess.

My aunties always choose only the straight and small ladies fingers; they swear that if one is bent it means there are grubs in it. In any case, they should be small, as large ladies fingers can become tough and woody.

Ingredients

300 g (10½ oz) ladies fingers (okra)	½ teaspoon ground cumin
2 teaspoons ground turmeric	½ teaspoon ground coriander
300 ml (10½ fl oz) vegetable oil	¼ teaspoon fenugreek seeds
1 small green chilli, finely chopped	1 tablespoon malt vinegar
½ teaspoon Maldive fish flakes (see Glossary)	200 ml (7 fl oz) coconut cream (see Glossary)
1 small onion, finely chopped	a pinch of roasted curry powder
1 sprig fresh curry leaves, leaves picked	(see page 36)
1 teaspoon chilli powder	SERVES 6

Method

Wash, trim and cut the ladies fingers on the diagonal into 3 cm (1¼ in) slices and toss in a bowl with the turmeric. Heat the oil in a deep-fryer or saucepan to 180°C (350°F) or until a cube of bread dropped in the oil browns in 15 seconds. Dust the excess turmeric off the ladies fingers and deep-fry them for 2 minutes or until golden, then drain on paper towels.

Place the remaining ingredients except the roasted curry powder in a heavy-based saucepan, bring to the boil and stir continuously for 5 minutes or until the sauce thickens. Add the fried ladies fingers, return to the boil, then season to taste with salt. Pour into a serving bowl and sprinkle with a little roasted curry powder. Do not stir in the curry powder.

Cucumber curry

This recipe uses the added boost of dry-roasted coconut which gives the curry a wonderful 'cooked on the open fire' taste and is also a thickening agent.

Ingredients

1 large telegraph (long), 2 white or
   3 Lebanese (short) cucumbers

2 tablespoons grated fresh coconut

1 teaspoon chilli powder

1 teaspoon ground coriander

½ teaspoon ground cumin

½ onion, finely chopped

1 sprig fresh curry leaves, leaves picked

½ teaspoon fennel seeds

2 cm (¾ in) piece cinnamon stick

¼ teaspoon ground turmeric

2 small green chillies, finely chopped

150 ml (5 fl oz) coconut milk (see Glossary)

SERVES 6

Method

Peel the cucumbers, cut in half lengthways, remove the seeds, then cut on the diagonal into 2 cm (¾ in) slices.

Place the coconut, chilli powder, coriander and cumin in a small heavy-based frying pan and shake over low heat for 8–10 minutes or until the coconut is dark golden.

Place the cucumber, coconut mixture and the remaining ingredients into a saucepan and simmer over medium heat for 7 minutes or until the cucumber is tender and the sauce has thickened.

Sunset at Gol Oya

The unspoilt East
TRINCOMALEE, one
—capable of accor
Trincomalee is well
splendid surroundin
also has a uniqu
in shallow waters
scattered over the
known as Swami
elephant-heads
multi-coloured tro
Apart from its
like Coral Cove,

Curried dahl soup

This is not the traditional dahl curry that we had at my grandmother's house, but it is the one we always use at home and in the restaurant. It is probably closer to an Indian dahl soup you would get with a Thali meal in southern India or northern Sri Lanka.

Ingredients

250 g (9 oz/1 cup) red lentils	5 cm (2 in) piece ginger, chopped
1 teaspoon ground turmeric	2 teaspoons cumin seeds
2 long dried red chillies	50 g (1¾ oz) ghee
1 red onion, finely chopped	1 sprig fresh curry leaves, leaves picked
1 vine-ripened tomato, chopped	2 teaspoons black mustard seeds
2 garlic cloves	**SERVES 6**

Method

Place the lentils, turmeric, chillies, onion, tomato and 1.25 litres (44 fl oz/5 cups) water in a saucepan, bring to the boil, then simmer gently for 15 minutes or until the lentils are tender and beginning to break up.

Meanwhile, place the garlic, ginger and cumin seeds in a mortar and pound with a pestle until a paste forms.

Heat the ghee in a small heavy-based frying pan over low–medium heat, add the curry leaves, mustard seeds and the spice paste and cook for 4 minutes or just until the seeds begin to pop and the mixture starts to brown. Pour the spice mixture into the lentil mixture, combine well and simmer for 4 minutes, then season to taste with salt.

Egg curry

A curry that my vegetarian Achi used to love, this is full of goodness and is really tasty. Deep-frying a peeled egg gives it a tofu-like exterior that absorbs the gravy.

Ingredients

6 eggs, plunged into boiling water for 5 minutes, then refreshed in iced water

750 ml (26 fl oz/3 cups) vegetable oil, for deep-frying

1 teaspoon chilli powder

1 teaspoon cumin seeds

½ teaspoon ground turmeric

1 tablespoon Maldive fish flakes (see Glossary)

1 onion, finely chopped

2 small green chillies, finely chopped

1 sprig fresh curry leaves, leaves picked

3 cm (1¼ in) piece of pandanus leaf

¼ teaspoon dill seeds

3 cm (1¼ in) piece cinnamon stick

350 ml (12 fl oz) coconut milk (see Glossary)

SERVES 6

Method

Carefully peel the cooked eggs, then prick them all over with a fork and lightly salt them.

Heat the vegetable oil to 180°C (350°F) or until a cube of bread dropped in the oil browns in 15 seconds. Deep-fry the eggs for 1 minute or until golden, then drain on paper towels.

Place all the remaining ingredients in a heavy-based saucepan and simmer over medium heat for 8 minutes or until the onion is soft and the sauce has thickened. Add the eggs and cook for another 5 minutes, then season to taste with salt.

Dahl and spinach curry

Ingredients

1 tablespoon ghee

4 shallots, finely chopped

1 garlic clove, finely chopped

1 sprig fresh curry leaves, leaves picked

125 g (4½ oz/½ cup) red lentils, washed
  and drained

2 small green chillies, finely chopped

½ teaspoon ground turmeric

700 ml (24 fl oz) coconut milk (see Glossary)

250 g (9 oz) English spinach leaves,
  picked, washed and roughly chopped

100 ml (3½ fl oz) coconut cream
  (see Glossary)

SERVES 6

Method

Heat the ghee in a heavy-based frying pan over low to medium heat, add the shallots and garlic and cook for 1–2 minutes or until just soft. Add the curry leaves and lentils and cook for another 3 minutes, then add the chilli, turmeric and coconut milk and cook for 8 minutes or until the dahl is soft and pulpy. Add the spinach and coconut cream and simmer for 3 minutes.

Season to taste with salt, and serve.

Pineapple curry

I love this typically Sri Lankan curry—although it sounds unusual it works very well. But it nearly started a riot while Karen and I were working in Fiji. Most of the men on the construction crews there were Fijian Indians, very particular about their south Indian-based curries. One night after I had cooked a Sri Lankan buffet for the resort guests we served the leftover curries to the Indian guys. Everything was fine until they ate some of the pineapple curry. I think they suspected that the kitchen staff were trying to wind them up—they all downed tools and went off to the general manager's office to complain. It took a long time for me to convince them that I only had their wellbeing in mind when I served them pineapple curry.

Things changed after that—they built their own kitchen next to their barracks and never had to deal with the resort kitchen again. This recipe is dedicated to Mani and the hard-working and immensely talented building team on Vatulele Island Resort, Fiji.

Ingredients

50 g (1¾ oz) ghee	1 teaspoon Maldive fish flakes (see Glossary)
1 onion, finely chopped	2 teaspoons dried chilli flakes
3 cm (1¼ in) piece pandanus leaf	1 teaspoon black mustard seeds
3 cm (1¼ in) piece lemongrass stem, bruised	¼ teaspoon ground turmeric
1 sprig fresh curry leaves, leaves picked	250 ml (9 fl oz/1 cup) coconut milk (see Glossary)
1 ripe pineapple, peeled, cored and cut into 2 cm (¾ in) pieces	¼ teaspoon fennel seeds, roasted and ground
3 cm (1¼ in) piece cinnamon stick	**SERVES 6**

Method

Heat the ghee in a heavy-based saucepan, add the onion, pandanus leaf, lemongrass and curry leaves and cook over low heat for 6–8 minutes or until the onion is translucent.

Add all the remaining ingredients except for the ground fennel, simmer for 5 minutes, then add the fennel, simmer for 4 minutes. Season to taste with salt and serve.

Beetroot curry

Deep pink in colour and retaining that unique beetroot flavour, this curry makes a stunning addition to a selection of dishes. While there is an urban myth that says beetroot leaves are poisonous, I have been making beetroot curry for years and I always incorporate the stems and leaves.

Ingredients

350 g (12 oz) small beetroots, washed, trimmed, stems reserved if desired

50 g (1¾ oz) ghee

1 large onion, finely chopped

2 small green chillies, finely chopped

3 cm (1¼ in) piece pandanus leaf

1 sprig fresh curry leaves, leaves picked

2 garlic cloves, thinly sliced

1 cinnamon stick

1 teaspoon ground coriander

1 teaspoon chilli powder

3 teaspoons white vinegar

1 teaspoon caster (superfine) sugar

200 ml (7 fl oz) coconut milk (see Glossary)

SERVES 6

Method

Cut the beetroots and stems (if using) into 1 cm (½ in) pieces.

Heat the ghee in a heavy-based saucepan over medium heat and cook the onion and green chilli for 6–8 minutes or until translucent. Add the pandanus leaf, curry leaves and garlic and cook for another 3 minutes or until fragrant.

Add the beetroot and the remaining ingredients, cover, and simmer over very low heat, stirring occasionally for 15–20 minutes or until the beetroot is tender. Season to taste and serve.

ACHI'S TREATS AND COMFORTERS

My grandmother had a deep knowledge of the Ayurvedic healing properties of many ingredients. The following recipes are a few of the special ones she would cook up if anybody deserved a treat or was not feeling the best.

Kola kanda

This creamy porridge of brown rice and coconut is a modern nutritionist's dream of a perfectly balanced meal and is particularly good for those with arthritis. Kola kanda is flavoured with the juice of green herbs such as polpala (*Aerva lantana*), hathawariya (*Asparagus falcatus*), gotukola (*Hydrocotyle asiatica*) or elabatu (*Solanum xanthocarpum*). This dish is delicious served steaming hot with a piece of palm sugar (jaggery).

Ingredients

200 g (7 oz/1 cup) brown or red rice

200 ml (7 fl oz) juice of one of the above herbs (or the juice of any green vegetable or culinary herbs)

4 pieces palm sugar (jaggery)

100 g (3 ½ oz) fresh grated coconut

SERVES 4

Method

Rinse the rice well, then place it in a heavy-based saucepan with 1.25 litres (44 fl oz/5 cups) of water. Simmer over medium heat for 25 minutes or until the rice breaks up and the soup is thick. You may have to add more water.

Add the coconut and cook for another 5 minutes, then remove from the heat, stir in the juice and serve hot with palm sugar.

Kiri bath

Kiri bath has a special place in Sri Lanka's culinary delights. A simple thick rice pudding made with coconut milk, then cut into diamond shapes, it is central to festive offerings and celebrations. Kiri bath plays an important part in New Year celebrations, and is included in birthday or anniversary meals, during wedding ceremonies and afterwards at the banquet. It is also used as a votive offering at temples.

Recently, my kids were asked to talk at school about their family traditions. They both said that on the first day of each month we always have kiri bath. It was a firm tradition in our ancestral home in Sri Lanka, and one that I have carried on.

I have mentioned condiments in earlier recipes. This is best eaten with lunu miris, some leftover fish or chicken curry gravy and a small sweet sugar banana. It is also good with a piece of rock palm sugar (jaggery), to balance the fiery lunu miris.

Ingredients

450 g (1 lb) raw long-grain white rice	150 ml (5 fl oz) coconut cream (see Glossary)
4 green cardamom pods, bruised	vegetable oil, for greasing
1.2 litres (42 fl oz) coconut milk (see Glossary)	**MAKES 16 PIECES**

Method

Wash and drain the rice, then put it in a heavy-based saucepan with the cardamom pods, coconut milk and 1 teaspoon of salt and cook, uncovered, stirring occasionally over high heat for 10 minutes or until the liquid has evaporated to the level of the rice. Add the coconut cream, cover and reduce the heat to low, then cook without stirring for 12 minutes or until the rice is cooked.

Using a wooden spoon, combine the hot rice well, then pour onto a 30 cm (12 in) tray or platter so that the rice is at least 5 cm (2 in) deep. Roll up a tea towel (dish towel), wrap it tightly in plastic wrap to resemble a rolling pin, then lightly grease it with vegetable oil and use to pat the hot rice mixture down until the top is even and smooth.

While the rice is still warm, cut into 6 cm (2½ in) diamonds and eat hot or cold.

Thambung hoddi

This is a rich, warming, spicy broth, especially valuable for those recovering from any kind of sickness. It is also given to women after they have given birth. My Dad made this soup for my Mum when she developed mastitis while she was breastfeeding David, my younger brother. Mum says that after a dose of thambung hoddi she regained her lost appetite very swiftly.

Ingredients

1 teaspoon cumin seeds

2 onions, coarsely sliced

2 small green chillies, coarsely chopped

3 teaspoons ground coriander

5 garlic cloves, coarsely chopped

1 sprig fresh curry leaves, leaves picked

5 black peppercorns

50 g (1¾ oz) tamarind concentrate

SERVES 4

Method

Place all the ingredients except the tamarind in a mortar and bruise with a pestle, then place them in a saucepan with the tamarind concentrate and 500 ml (17 fl oz/2 cups) of water. Bring to the boil, then simmer for 15 minutes. Remove from the heat and allow to stand for 1 hour, then strain through a fine sieve. Discard the solids and drink the broth.

Kothamalli

Kothamalli is Tamil for coriander. It is also a drink rich in healing properties—the ginger works on colds and fevers while the coriander seeds, cinnamon and ginger all help to warm the body during times of sickness.

Whenever I feel the onset of a cold, I brew up some kothamalli.

Ingredients

50 g (1¾ oz) coriander seeds .... 2 slices young ginger ....

5 cm (2 in) piece of cinnamon stick .... **SERVES 4**

Method

Rinse the coriander seeds, then place in a dry frying pan and cook over low heat until lightly toasted.

Put all the ingredients in a saucepan with 600 ml (21 fl oz) of water and simmer over medium heat for 15 minutes, then strain and serve with or without sugar.

On the
road

chapter four
On the road

IN SRI LANKA, FRESH REGIONAL AND SEASONAL FOODS ARE ENJOYED BY ALL. ROAD TRIPS ARE POPULAR, AND AS PEOPLE TRAVEL ACROSS THE COUNTRY THEY STOP TO EAT AT TEAHOUSES AND BOUTIQUES (AS THEY ARE CALLED). LUNCH PACKETS, STREET FOOD AND THE GREAT TASTES OF FOODS FROM THE ISLAND'S DIFFERENT ETHNIC GROUPS CAN ALL BE SAVOURED.

As the sun sets, the hopper shops and rotti stalls come to life, offering a wide range of delicious treats: kottu rotti, egg hoppers, masalawadde and gothamba rotti, to mention just a few. The clanging of the griddle can be heard everywhere as kottu rotti is chopped, while people in small tin sheds fry masalawadde.

I will always remember going to these kinds of shops with my Dad when I was a child. Someone brings you a plate full of spicy delicacies—when you've finished eating, they simply count how many are left and charge you for what you've had.

Each region has its own special food.

In the south there is kalu dodol which is made with palm treacle, cashew nuts and cardamom. This wonderful jelly-like pudding is especially sought after by the disciples who leave the holy city of Kataragama after their pilgrimage. Making kalu dodol is a very labour-intensive process; most people buy it from roadside shops rather than making it themselves.

The south is also famous for buffalo curd (yoghurt) usually made on small farms from fresh unpasteurised buffalo milk. The milk is heated and then cultured with a teaspoonful of curd from the previous batch. No one knows how the first batch was made but it dates back hundreds of years.

Another southern speciality is palm treacle or panni which comes from the kittul palm. It is produced by cutting the end off the flower of the palm and placing an earthenware pot over it to catch the juice. When it is fermented it is called toddy and can be used as a raising agent instead of yeast. This luscious syrup is smoked after being boiled until thick, which gives it a delicious, unusual flavour. The syrup is greatly prized for the national treat called simply 'curds and honey' (see picture page 226), the curds being rich, firm yoghurt made from buffalo milk and topped with a thick layer of yellow cream.

When boiled down even further, the syrup of the kittul palm is reduced to a heavy, moist palm sugar similar to that used in Thai cooking. It is sold in wide-mouthed jars from which it is spooned. This palm sugar ranges in colour from almost white to pale honey-gold to deep, dark brown, with a variable consistency.

For those who like a drink, roadside stalls also sell toddy and arrack, alcoholic drinks made from the nectar of the coconut flower. All along the tropical shores of the Indian Ocean, toddy tappers climb coconut trees to collect the toddy (itself mildly alcoholic) which is placed into traditional wooden barrels and transported to the distillery to be made into arrack.

There are pilgrimages to holy sites around the country; my most vivid memories are from Kataragama, the holy city in the south where people of all religions come to cleanse themselves in the Kelani River and make offerings to the gods of all religions.

For me the most symbolic form of offering involved buying a coconut and a cube of camphor from one of the many colourful stands surrounding the main temple complex. We would light the camphor and place it on top of the coconut. While the camphor burns you make a wish and just before it goes out you smash the coconut on a black stone in front of the temple. If your wish comes true you have to return to the holy site and make an offering.

To get to the temple you have to cross the Kelani via a footbridge, below which are hundreds of people bathing in the river with three or four of the temple elephants. These lucky elephants are washed and groomed with coconut husks by their mahouts and a few helpers. At night they are dressed in colourful robes and ornaments and lead a noisy procession of thousands of people around the temple—it's quite a spectacle.

A lot of people come from the east and far north of the country, some walking all the way. I have vivid memories of processions of pilgrims going past my grandmother's house. Some Hindu people will go to extreme lengths to show their devotion or engage in cleansing rituals. I remember seeing devotees suspended by large hooks skewered through the flesh in their backs in a rickety cart drawn by other devotees; others had large steel rods through their mouths and tongues or would roll along the ground for the entire journey.

On one occasion when I was five or six our whole family went to the Kelani River and stayed in the temple grounds in a dormitory with about 500 other people. My father wanted to offer prayers to Lord Kataragama asking for blessings on his new business venture, the foundry where he would make hard-to-get parts for machinery.

We were all served a simple but memorable meal. Sitting with our backs against the walls of the dormitory's narrow corridors, each of us had a banana leaf—an eco friendly plate—on the floor in front of our feet. The Hindu priests rolled giant pots on wheels through the corridors, dishing out rice, dahl and vegetables. I don't know if it was because I was hungry, but it tasted fantastic!

When I awoke the next morning there was noise and action everywhere and I was alone. Upset and crying for my Mum and Dad, I wandered out into the throng of thousands of people; eventually the kind pilgrims reunited me with my family. In 2007 I went back to visit the Kataragama temple grounds and realised what a miracle it was that I had been reunited with them.

There is another significant pilgrimage site in the south called Adams Peak, or Siri Pade in Sinhalese. High in the mountains, right at the top of a few thousand uneven and slippery stone steps, is a single footprint, revered by Buddhists as the footprint of Lord Buddha (although the Christians and Muslims have other explanations for it). Our whole family made this pilgrimage one year; my Mum says that as a six-year-old I climbed to the top totally unassisted. All of these things are possible when you are in the right frame of mind—I remember my aunties and cousins saying that if you keep your thoughts pure and believe you are able to climb the mountain, you can. There's a lot to be said for the simple faith of little children.

I have looked at all the hurdles in my life as my own Adams Peaks. I feel that when, as a six-year-old, I reached the top of that sacred mountain, my determination to succeed in everything I did was cemented into my mind. Subconsciously, I use it every day—the spiritual connection I made as the sun rose that day has remained a key part of me.

Sri Lanka is full of wondrous religious and historical sites, guaranteed to inspire travellers with joy and amazement.

In the central northern region sits Sigiriya, the rock fortress built by King Kasyapa in the fifth century AD. With its extraordinary structures and artwork, it is listed as a world heritage site.

Anuradhapura in the north is one of the ancient capitals of Sri Lanka and is now an historic site spanning more than 40 square kilometres. It is held particularly sacred by Buddhists and the entire area is dotted with Buddha statues and the remnants of great Buddhist architecture.

Polonnaruwa, also in the north, is another of Sri Lanka's ancient capitals and was ruled and held by three different kings: Vijayabahu (1055–1110); Parakramabahu (1153–1186); and Nissanka Malla (1187–1196). All three contributed to the architecture of this site but it is most famous for its massive tank and irrigation system, spanning 2400 hectares and able to irrigate 75,000 hectares of rice paddies.

Dambulla in central Sri Lanka is a cave monastery that has been in operation for over 2000 years. It has five caves with depictions of the lord Buddha. As a kid, I visited Dambulla and I still remember the cheeky monkeys stealing anything that was not properly secured. The views from the top are amazing.

In the centre of the island is Kandy, known as Maha Nuwara (the great city), surrounded and protected by mountain ranges. The seat of the kings, it was unassailable for both the Dutch and Portuguese invaders who tried many times to conquer it. Kandy is home to the sacred relic of Lord Buddha's tooth, brought there more than 1600 years ago by a princess from Orissa in India. The Temple of the Tooth hosts the annual Esala Perahera, a famous and colourful pageant said to bring the rains, which culminates in a grand parade on the night of the August full moon.

There are so many places to see around this beautiful gem of an island. You can catch a train up to the hill country which is covered in tea plantations and has a cool climate and amazing views.

My Uncle Lionel was a train driver; he had six daughters and was always asking me if I wanted to come and live with him. When our family travelled to the country by train he would have a compartment reserved for us. I was my uncle's favourite nephew and he had a special treat for me on these trips. Once the train was out of Colombo and starting to climb into the hill country he would stop the train, run down the tracks, collect me from our carriage and take me into the engine compartment where I got to drive the train and hoot the horn. It was amazing! I felt like I was king of the world. When I finally fell asleep in the engineer's seat he or one of the other guys would carry me back to my family.

As a small boy I made that trip by myself a few times to stay with my cousins who were stationed in the hill country. My only memory of food there was of the beautiful avocados which had red skins and were creamy and tasty.

LUNCH PACKETS AND SHORT EATS

Short trips around the country are very popular in Sri Lanka—everyone goes on road trips together, either crammed into government and private coaches or using their own transport. We were fortunate enough to have a large van, so we would squeeze in as many people as we could and off we'd go.

The food was very important and lunch packets were carefully prepared the night before, with Achi and my Mum and all the aunties very busy. A lunch packet was a ritual: firstly, we would make the curries, often Ambul thial, a dry tuna curry (see page 85), and then we would cook the rice. This was normally samba rice which is a pungent, small-grained rice known as 'chicken teeth'. We usually added dahl and vegetables as well.

We would collect clean untorn banana leaves which we waved over an open fire until they softened. These were laid on top of newspaper and the rice and curry was then placed on top of the banana leaf to be wrapped and tied.

When these lunch packets were opened they were delicious—the flavours
of the curry and the banana leaf had mingled and the food was a treat to eat.

We often took fruit as well—ripe mangoes and pineapples, peeled, and
seasoned with a fifty-fifty mix of salt and chilli; my mouth waters just thinking
of it. This went very well with the chickpeas mixed with chilli and fresh shards of
coconut that were sold on the beach.

'Short eats' was a term originally used to describe sandwiches and savouries
eaten around or after 6pm. Today they can be anything from a pre-dinner canapé
to a small snack with tea while on the road. They are varied and can range from
sweet to excruciatingly spicy.

The following recipes reflect the kind of food found everywhere along the
road in Sri Lanka but they are just as good cooked at home and eaten as snacks
with a drink at the end of the day.

Devilled cashew nuts

This is a classic hotel 'beer on the balcony' treat. I like to judge a hotel's kitchen by their devilled cashews.

Ingredients

100 ml (3½ fl oz) vegetable oil	½ teaspoon salt
300 g (10½ oz) raw unsalted cashew nuts	½ teaspoon black pepper powder
2 sprigs fresh curry leaves, leaves picked	
½ teaspoon chilli powder	**SERVES 4**

Method

Heat the oil in a heavy-based frying pan just until a light smoke haze becomes visible. Add the cashews and stir for 3 minutes or until golden. Add the curry leaves and cook for another 30 seconds.

Pour the cashews and curry leaves into a sieve placed over a heat-proof bowl to drain the oil, then drain on paper towels. Place in a bowl with the chilli powder and salt and toss to combine well. Serve with a good cold beer.

Roasted peanuts

Roasted peanuts from roadside stalls always tasted so good, but you can make them just as well at home.

Ingredients

150 g (5½ oz) rock salt

250 g (9 oz) fresh raw peanuts in their skins

SERVES 4

Method

Place the salt in a wok in a well-ventilated kitchen or outside on a barbecue flat plate. Cook over high heat until the salt begins to crackle. Be very careful not to touch the crackling salt as by this stage it will be over 300°C (570°F).

Add the peanuts to the salt and stir continuously for 5 minutes or until the skins become crisp and a roasted peanut aroma develops. Pour the nut and salt mixture into a coarse seive and shake until the salt is removed.

Serve in a bowl with a pre-dinner drink or simply poured into a newspaper cone.

Pineapple or mango with salt and chilli

This dish is ideal with arrack, Sri Lanka's national liquor. It is also sold on the beach and at the island's many historic sites. As kids we would climb our own mango tree and get one of our aunties to make it for us.

Ingredients

1 teaspoon fine salt

1 teaspoon chilli powder

1 teaspoon ground black pepper

1 ripe pineapple or 3 green mangoes

SERVES 4

Method

Combine the salt, chilli powder and pepper. Peel the fruit and cut it into fingers, thread it onto skewers, then sprinkle with the chilli salt mixture. Allow to stand for 30 minutes before serving.

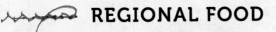

REGIONAL FOOD

We used to stay at a lodge near Arugam Bay in the south-east of the country. It was a place of great natural beauty and host to a most amazing butterfly migration once a year. Thousands of butterflies head inland towards Adams Peak late every year during the North-East Monsoon period when all the plants are green and fresh. They lay their eggs among the thick foliage which provides a constant food supply for the emerging caterpillars. The butterflies come in seemingly endless hordes, winging their way a metre or so above the ground; the migration goes on for hours, days or weeks on end. In home gardens, on the roads, over paddy fields, across irrigation reservoirs, and even inside homes, they flutter like leaves fanned by the breeze. We used to play in the grounds of the lodge and they would stick to our skin.

This lodge was also an unofficial hunting lodge where really bad hunters with shocking aim used to come and try their luck around the borders of the national parks. There were deer, wild boar and wild chickens to hunt. Dad was totally against killing anything and never partook in the sport; while he stayed at the lodge we kids all happily jumped in the jeep and went off with the hunters and their guides, the sons of the lodge owner.

The lodge owner was so into hunting that he named his four sons after guns: there was Remington, Winchester, Ruger and Walther. Remington was my favourite; he was the skinner and an excellent guide. He led the 'great hunters' to many game animals and so many times they screamed with delight because they thought they had shot something. But we could never find the beasts. Returning the next day in daylight, we usually found the bullet holes 2 metres above the ground in a tree. Much to my Dad's relief the animals were quite safe with those guys.

We did eat some amazing food at that lodge, though; the chicken and wild boar curries were the best anyone had tasted.

Wild boar or pork curry

Ingredients

900 g (2 lb) pork belly with the bone in,
  cut into 2.5 cm (1 in) pieces

1 teaspoon cumin seeds, dry roasted
  and ground

1 teaspoon fennel seeds, dry roasted
  and ground

½ teaspoon ground turmeric

2 cm (¾ in) piece ginger, thinly sliced

2 teaspoons dried chilli flakes

2 pieces Goroka (see Glossary)

1 cinnamon stick

2 tablespoons raw long-grain rice,
  finely pounded

2 cloves

4 green cardamom pods, bruised

1 sprig fresh curry leaves, leaves picked

2 tablespoons vegetable oil

1 red onion, peeled and finely chopped

5 garlic cloves, thinly sliced

SERVES 6

Method

Combine the pork in a bowl with all the ingredients except the oil, onions and garlic. Cover and allow to stand for 1 hour.

Heat the oil in a large heavy-based saucepan over medium heat, add the onion and cook for 6–8 minutes or until translucent. Add the pork mixture, garlic and 250 ml (9 fl oz/1 cup) of water and simmer over low heat for 25 minutes or until the meat is tender and the gravy is thick. Season to taste with salt.

Prawn curry

There was a lagoon on the other side of the lodge at Arugam Bay that opened out to one of the best surf spots in the world. At night the prawn fishermen used to come here with massive torches made of cloth wound around a bamboo pole. These were suspended over the lagoon while the fishermen cast hand nets into the water. Each time the nets came back full of large jumbo prawns with long claws and brilliant blue bodies. The prawn curry from this lodge is one of the best we have tasted.

Ingredients

500 g (1 lb 2 oz) raw medium prawns,
peeled, with the tails intact (reserve
the heads)

150 g (5½ oz) coconut powder mixed
with 300 ml (10½ fl oz) hot water

50 g (1¾ oz) ghee

1 onion, finely chopped

2 garlic cloves, thinly sliced

5 cm (2 in) piece ginger, thinly sliced

1 sprig fresh curry leaves, leaves picked

5 cm (2 in) piece pandanus leaf

1 cinnamon stick

2 cloves

2 green cardamom pods, bruised

½ teaspoon fenugreek seeds

1 teaspoon chilli powder

¼ teaspoon ground turmeric

1 teaspoon ground cumin

2 teaspoons ground coriander

½ teaspoon paprika

1 teaspoon fish curry powder (see page 39)

2 long green chillies, finely chopped

juice of ½ a lime

SERVES 6

Method

Rinse the reserved prawn heads well and discard as much of the soft matter as possible. Place the reserved prawn heads and 200 ml (7 fl oz) of water in a food processor and blend until a smooth paste forms. Strain it through a fine sieve, extracting as much liquid as possible. Discard the solids, then combine the paste with the coconut milk.

Heat the ghee in a heavy-based saucepan over medium heat, add the onion, garlic, ginger, curry leaves and pandanus leaf and cook over low heat for 6–8 minutes or until the onions are translucent.

Add the prawns and all the remaining ingredients except for the prawn paste and the lime juice and stir continuously for 5 minutes. Add 300 ml (10½ fl oz) of water to the pan, combine well and cook for another 7 minutes, then reduce the heat to low. Stir in the prawn paste and cook for another 8 minutes or until the flavours are well combined, the sauce has thickened and the 'raw curry' flavour has gone. Do not let the curry boil or it will split. Remove from the heat and stand the curry for 1 hour to allow the flavours to combine. To serve, add a squeeze of lime and gently reheat.

Krill sambal

One of my uncles lived in the south coast town of Kosgoda. He was married to a German lady, and Mum and she were friends—my uncle and his wife had three daughters and we all got on well. Their house was on a cinnamon and copra plantation which was a wonderland for kids: we ran wild through the plantation and swam in the lagoon that bordered the property. The lagoon was full of millions of krill that would find their way into every nook and cranny if you were unlucky enough to swim into them but when caught and cooked, made a fantastic sambal.

Ingredients

200 g (7 oz) krill	½ fresh coconut, grated
2 pieces Goroka (see Glossary)	20 g (¾ oz) ghee
150 ml (5 fl oz) coconut milk (see Glossary)	¼ teaspoon dried chilli flakes
a pinch of ground turmeric	1 sprig fresh curry leaves, leaves picked
¼ teaspoon roasted fenugreek seeds	juice of ½ a lime
1 small green chilli, finely chopped	
2 small onions, finely chopped	SERVES 6

Method

Wash the krill and Goroka together, drain and place in a heavy-based saucepan. Add the coconut milk, turmeric, fenugreek seeds, green chilli and half the chopped onion and bring to the boil over medium heat, then reduce the heat to low and simmer for 5 minutes or until the onion is translucent. Add the grated coconut and cook for another 5 minutes.

Meanwhile, heat the ghee in a heavy-based frying pan over medium heat and cook the remaining onion, dried chilli flakes and curry leaves for another 5 minutes or until the onion is golden. Add to the krill mixture and cook for another 3 minutes, then stir in the lime juice and season to taste with salt.

There is a photograph of krill sambal on page 174.

ETHNIC SPECIALITIES

In this section I have focused on food that represents each of Sri Lanka's three major ethnic groups: Sinhalese, Tamil and Muslim. I have included some of my favourite recipes from each of them and you will also find some of their other specialities throughout the book.

SINHALESE
Sinhala-speaking Sri Lankans make up about 75 percent of the population and are mostly Buddhists. Their food is generally very nutritious and includes the hoppers for which Sri Lankan cuisine is so well known.

Fish cutlets

These are delicious hot or cold and go really well with a beer. They should be quite spicy but you can adjust the heat by increasing or decreasing the amount of chilli.

Ingredients

350 g (12 oz) piece of skinless bonito or tuna, cut into 4 cm (1½ in) pieces

200 g (7 oz) pontiac potatoes, peeled and cut into 2 cm (¾ in) pieces

½ teaspoon freshly ground black pepper

1 litre (35 fl oz/4 cups) vegetable oil

1 onion, finely chopped

1 sprig fresh curry leaves, leaves picked

¼ teaspoon ground cumin

½ teaspoon chilli powder

¼ teaspoon coriander powder

3 small green chillies, finely chopped

1 teaspoon sea salt

plain (all-purpose) flour, for dusting

2 eggs, lightly beaten

75 g (2½ oz/¾ cup) fine dry breadcrumbs

MAKES 16

Method

Sprinkle the fish and potatoes with the black pepper, then place them in a steamer and steam for 10 minutes or until the potatoes are tender.

Meanwhile, heat 2 tablespoons of the oil in a heavy-based frying pan over low heat and cook the onion, curry leaves, cumin, chilli powder and coriander powder for 6–8 minutes or until the onion is soft but not brown.

Coarsely mash the potato and fish in a bowl, add the fresh chilli, onion mixture and salt and combine well. Divide the mixture into 16 portions, then shape each portion in the palm of your hand to make small discs.

Dust the fish cutlets in the flour, then dip in the egg and coat with breadcrumbs. Place on a baking paper-lined tray and stand for 10 minutes. Heat the remaining oil in a deep-fryer or large heavy-based saucepan to 180°C (350°F) or until a cube of bread dropped in the oil browns in 15 seconds. Deep-fry the cutlets in batches until they are golden, then drain on paper towels and serve hot or at room temperature.

Mutton rolls

Ingredients

650 g (1 lb 7 oz) russet potatoes, scrubbed	6 large mint leaves, finely chopped
300 g (10½ oz) minced (ground) lamb	2 small green chillies, finely chopped
2 tablespoons malt vinegar	125 g (4½ oz/1 cup) plain (all-purpose) flour
1 teaspoon sea salt	2 eggs, lightly beaten
2 teaspoons freshly ground black pepper	165 g (5¾ oz/1¾ cups) fine dry breadcrumbs
1 litre (35 fl oz/4 cups) vegetable oil	
2 onions, finely chopped	**MAKES ABOUT 20 ROLLS**

Method

Place the unpeeled potatoes in a large saucepan, cover with lightly salted water and simmer until tender. Drain. When cool enough to handle, peel and coarsely mash the potatoes.

Meanwhile, combine the lamb, vinegar, salt and pepper in a bowl and allow to stand for 10 minutes.

Heat 2 tablespoons of the oil in a heavy-based frying pan over high heat, add the lamb mixture and cook, stirring regularly and breaking up the mince with the back of a wooden spoon, for 8 minutes or until most of the liquid has evaporated. Add the onion, mint and chilli and cook, stirring continuously, for 5 minutes. Remove and place in a sieve to drain any excess liquid.

Using a piece of plastic wrap or a lightly oiled banana leaf, place a heaped tablespoon of potato mash in the centre and flatten into a rectangle about 8 x 10 cm (3¼ x 4 in). Place 2 teaspoons of mince mixture along the centre and, starting at one long side, roll up tightly and place on a baking paper-lined tray. Refrigerate for 30 minutes, then carefully remove the wrapping from the rolls. Dust each roll in the flour, then dip in the egg and coat with breadcrumbs.

Heat the remaining oil in a deep-fryer or large heavy-based saucepan to 180°C (350°F) or until a cube of bread dropped in the oil browns in 15 seconds. Deep-fry the rolls in batches until they are crisp and golden, then drain on paper towels and serve hot or cold.

Egg hoppers

Although this dish is eaten throughout Sri Lanka and is available at the most basic boutiques, it is one recipe that nobody can agree on. The sought-after result is one where the sides are crisp and the centre is aerated and soft. My conclusion, after much research and many conversations on this topic, is that the recipe becomes very personal—you will need to tweak it until you get the result you desire.

In Western countries one vital ingredient is unavailable—toddy. Toddy or Rah, obtained by tapping the young flowers of the coconut palm, has been the traditional beverage of Sri Lankans for over twenty-five centuries. Yeast in the sweet sap ferments the sugar into alcohol, but I have found an alternative that works as well. It's very simple—a piece of sougdough bread.

In Sri Lanka everyone uses 'appa soda' when they can't get toddy; it is sold in 100 gram (3½ oz) lots in plastic bags. No one seems to have any idea what is in it. I suspect it is bicarbonate of soda but have not tested my theory—I was unwilling to carry 100 grams of white powder in an unmarked plastic bag when I returned to Sydney as I did not want to be the last one out of the airport that day.

The best breakfast hopper is made by pouring a lightly beaten egg into the centre just before steaming the hopper—served with some gravy from a great chicken curry, this is one of Sri Lanka's many gems. A great dessert is made by adding 150 g (5½ oz) of palm sugar (jaggery) or honey to the batter after it has fermented, and serving the hoppers with bananas.

Hoppers are traditionally made in a hopper pan which is essentially a small wok with handles. Alternatively, use a small non-stick frying pan.

Good luck with this one—once you've perfected it you will have unlocked the treasure of one of Sri Lanka's best dishes.

1 large coconut, coconut water reserved

1 large slice sourdough, crusts removed

400 ml (14 fl oz) second extract of
coconut, made from grated flesh (see
page 247 of Glossary for instructions).

500 g (1 lb 2 oz) rice flour, sifted

1 teaspoon caster (superfine) sugar

¼ teaspoon bicarbonate of soda

a pinch of salt

200 ml (7 fl oz) first extract of coconut
(see Glossary)

vegetable oil, for greasing

MAKES 15 HOPPERS

Method

To make the coconut milk, crack the coconut, reserve the coconut water and grate the flesh to use for the coconut milk extracts (see page 247 of Glossary). Set aside.

Place the crustless bread, reserved coconut water and the second extract of coconut in a bowl and blend until smooth. Mix together the rice flour, sugar, and bicarbonate of soda over the liquid bread mixture and whisk until a smooth but thick batter forms.

Cover the bowl and stand it in a warm place for 6–8 hours or until the batter mixture is frothy and increased in volume. The standing time will vary considerably depending on the room temperature—the warmer the better. Remember it is nearly always 30°C (85°F) and 90 percent humidity in Sri Lanka.

Just before cooking, stir in a pinch of salt and the first extract of coconut.

Heat a small non-stick frying pan over high heat, wipe the pan lightly with oil, then pour in a 60 ml (2 fl oz/¼ cup) ladleful of mixture. Swirl the mixture to coat the sides of the pan, leaving a small pool of mixture in the centre. Cover the pan with a lid and steam the hopper for 2–3 minutes or until the centre is firm and the sides are golden and crisp. Slide out and keep the cooked hoppers warm. Repeat the process until all the batter has been used.

String hoppers

String hoppers are made from a hot-water dough of rice meal or wheat flour pressed out in circlets from a string mould onto little wicker mats, then steamed. Light and lacy, string hoppers make a mouth-watering meal with curry and sambal. String hopper moulds and mats are available from your Sri Lankan grocer.

My preference is for wheat flour; the issue with this is that you have to steam the flour first. Alternatively you can buy the flour steamed, ground and strained. Using rice flour basically gives you a rice noodle in a different shape.

Ingredients

450 g (1 lb) plain (all-purpose) flour or
rice flour

MAKES 15 HOPPERS

Method

If using wheat flour, wrap it in a clean tea towel (dish towel), place the bundle in a bamboo steamer and steam for 1 hour. While still hot, unwrap the flour, process it in a food processor until smooth, then pass it through a fine sieve.

Bring 500 ml (17 fl oz/2 cups) of water to the boil, pour it into a large heatproof bowl and allow it to cool slightly. Add the flour and a pinch of salt and stir until a soft, pliable dough forms—the dough should be a little softer than playdough. Working in batches, place a little dough in the string hopper mould, then squeeze out the dough onto the mats, starting in the centre and working outwards, then back in again to make an even double layer of dough. Stack the mats on top of each other and steam for 3–5 minutes.

Serve immediately with curry and sambal.

Crab curry

This recipe is a favourite of mine. It calls for murunga (drumstick leaves) but it can be made without them. Crab curry is delicious served with krill sambal (see page 160).

Ingredients

2 live mud crabs, about 1.25 kg
  (2 lb 12 oz) each

400 ml (14 fl oz) coconut milk (see Glossary)

1 piece Goroka (see Glossary)

1 tablespoon chilli powder

2 teaspoons cumin seeds, roasted
  and ground

5 cm (2 in) piece cinnamon stick

1 teaspoon fenugreek seeds

¼ teaspoon ground turmeric

50 g (1¾ oz) ghee

3 small onions, finely chopped

2 cm (¾ in) piece ginger, peeled and finely
  chopped

1 sprig curry leaves, leaves picked

5 cm (2 in) piece pandanus leaf

1 lemongrass stem, bruised

3 small green chillies, finely chopped

¼ teaspoon dill seeds

30 g (1 oz/1 cup) (loosely packed
  coriander leaves

1 sprig murunga (drumstick leaves)

juice of ½ a lime

SERVES 6

Method

Put the crabs in the freezer for 1 hour to immobilise them. Pull off the top shells, pull out the spongy grey gills and remove the guts. Chop each crab into 6 pieces, then crack the large claws but leave them attached. Place the crab pieces in a large bowl with the coconut milk, Goroka, chilli powder, cumin, cinnamon, fenugreek and turmeric. Combine well and allow to stand for 20 minutes.

Heat the ghee in a wide heavy-based saucepan over high heat, add the onion, ginger, curry leaves, pandanus leaf, lemongrass and chillies and cook for 5 minutes or until the onion is golden. Add the dill seeds and cook for another 2 minutes, then add the crab mixture. Cover and simmer for 12 minutes or until the crab is just cooked through and the sauce has thickened. Stir in the coriander, murunga and lime juice, and season to taste with salt.

TAMIL FOOD

Tamils make up about 18 percent of Sri Lanka's population and most of them are Hindus. Tamil food is typically simple and nutritious with a focus on rice and curry.

Thosai

This dish, a kind of very thin pancake, is wonderful for breakfast with some sambal or leftover curry from the night before. It is traditionally made using a flat pan called a tava, which are available from Indian grocers, but you can use a non-stick frying pan.

You will need to start this recipe the day before you intend to serve it.

Ingredients

250 g (9 oz) urad dahl (black mung beans)

1 teaspoon fenugreek seeds

125 g (4½ oz) Samba rice (see Glossary)

750 g (1 lb 10 oz/3¾ cups) white long-grain rice

1 teaspoon vegetable oil, plus extra for brushing

2 onions, finely chopped

1 sprig fresh curry leaves, leaves picked

2 long dried red chillies, broken (optional)

¼ teaspoon cumin seeds

¼ teaspoon black mustard seeds

SERVES 6

Method

Place the urad dahl and fenugreek seeds in one container and the rice in another, cover both with plenty of cold water and allow to stand for at least 6 hours.

Using a blender, process each of the drained soaked ingredients, gradually adding small quantities of cold water to make thick pastes (they must not be runny). Combine the two pastes in a container which is at least twice the size of the combined paste mixture, and add a pinch of salt. Cover and stand overnight in a cool place, but do not refrigerate.

Heat the oil in a small heavy-based frying pan over medium heat. Add the onion, curry leaves and dried chillies and cook for 5 minutes or until the onion is golden. Add the cumin and mustard seeds and cook just until the mustard seeds begin to pop, then pour the onion mixture into the fermented batter.

Heat a tava, flat griddle or non-stick frying pan over high heat and wipe it lightly with oil. Place a 60 ml (2 fl oz/¼ cup) ladleful of batter onto the tava and smooth it with the base of the ladle to create a thin pancake. Cook for 2 minutes, then turn and cook for another 1 minute or until the pancakes are golden and crisp. Serve hot.

Sambar

A lentil-based dish, sambar is usually served with steamed rice for breakfast or lunch.

Ingredients

50 g (1¾ oz/¼ cup) chana dahl
  (yellow lentils)

2 tablespoons vegetable oil

½ teaspoon black mustard seeds

a pinch of asafoetida

25 red shallots, peeled

2 small green chillies, halved lengthways

2 cups vegetables cut into 3 cm (1¼ in)
  pieces—include 25 g (1 oz) eggplant
  (aubergine), 50 g (1¾ oz) carrots,
  50 g (1¾ oz) green beans, 50 g (1¾ oz)
  pumpkin, 50 g (1¾ oz) sweet potato

50 ml (1½ fl oz) tamarind pulp, soaked

in 80 ml (2½ fl oz/1/1⁄3 cup) warm water
  for 10 minutes, strained, fibres discarded

1½ teaspoons finely grated palm sugar
  (jaggery) or brown sugar

½ teaspoon fenugreek seeds, dry roasted

MASALA

1 teaspoon urad dahl (black mung beans)

3 long dried red chillies, broken

1½ tablespoons coriander seeds

¼ fresh coconut, finely grated

5 sprigs fresh curry leaves, leaves picked

SERVES 6

Method

Place the chana dahl in a saucepan, cover well with cold water and simmer over medium heat for 15 minutes, drain, then mash.

Meanwhile, for the masala, heat 1 tablespoon of the oil in a heavy-based saucepan over medium heat, add ½ a teaspoon of urad dahl and stir for 5 minutes or until it begins to brown. Add the dried chilli, coriander seeds, coconut and most of the curry leaves and cook for another 4 minutes or until the coconut is a golden brown. Remove the pan from the heat, allow the mixture to cool, then place in a mortar, add 3 tablespoons water and grind with a pestle until a fine paste forms.

Heat the remaining oil in a large heavy-based frying pan over medium heat, add the mustard seeds and cook for 2–3 minutes or just until the seeds begin to pop. Add the remaining urad dahl and the asafoetida and cook for 1 minute, then add the shallots, green chillies, ½ teaspoon salt and the remaining the curry leaves.

Add the vegetables and cook for 5 minutes or until aromatic, then add 1 tablespoon of water, cover and cook for another 10 minutes or until the vegetables are cooked but still firm. Add the tamarind liquid, palm sugar and fenugreek seeds and cook for another 5 minutes or until the raw aroma of the tamarind disappears. Add the mashed lentils and the masala, combine well, adding a little water if mixture seems to dry, then simmer for 5 minutes. Season to taste with salt.

Vadai

Vadai and bondas are great snack foods that are sold in the roadside boutiques piping hot with tea cappuccino.

Vadai is also known as Point Pedro Vadai—Point Pedro is the northernmost tip of Sri Lanka. To give them a seafood cracker flavour, you can push a whole small peeled green prawn into each of the balls before shaping them into discs.

You will need to start this recipe the night before you plan to eat the vadai.

Ingredients

250 g (9 oz) urad dahl (black mung beans), soaked in cold water overnight

120 g (4¼ oz/2 cups) finely grated fresh coconut

100 g (3½ oz) finely chopped onions

2 garlic cloves, crushed with 1 teaspoon salt

3 cm (1¼ in) piece ginger, grated

2 small green chillies, finely chopped

10 fresh curry leaves, coarsely chopped

½ teaspoon ground turmeric

270 g (9½ oz/1½ cups) roasted white rice flour (available from Asian grocers)

1 teaspoon chilli powder

1 teaspoon cumin seeds

1 teaspoon salt

1 litre (35 fl oz/4 cups) vegetable oil, for deep-frying

MAKES ABOUT 30

Method

Drain the urad dahl, then place it in a bowl with all the other ingredients except the oil. Combine well to make a thick paste.

Heat the oil in a deep-fryer or large deep saucepan to 180°C (350°F) or until a cube of bread dropped into the oil browns in 15 seconds. Working in batches, shape teaspoonfuls of the paste into balls, then flatten them out into discs approximately 1 cm (½ in) thick.

Deep-fry the vadai for 4–6 minutes or until golden, and cooked inside. Drain on paper towels and serve immediately.

Bonda

Ingredients

250 g (9 oz) russet potatoes, scrubbed

1 litre (35 fl oz/4 cups) vegetable oil

½ teaspoon black mustard seeds

¼ teaspoon ground turmeric

2 long dried red chillies

2 small onions, finely chopped

1 small green chilli, finely chopped

2 sprigs fresh curry leaves, leaves picked

BATTER

110 g (3¾ oz/1 cup) chana besan (chickpea) flour

1 tablespoon white rice flour

a pinch of bicarbonate of soda (baking soda)

¼ teaspoon ground turmeric

MAKES ABOUT 20

Method

Put the unpeeled potatoes in a saucepan of cold salted water, bring to the boil and simmer until the potatoes are tender. Drain. When cool enough to handle, peel the potatoes and mash them coarsely.

Heat 2 tablespoons of the oil in a heavy-based saucepan over medium heat, add the mustard seeds, turmeric and dried red chilli and cook for 1 minute, then add the onion and green chilli. Cook for another 6–8 minutes or until the onion is golden. Add the mashed potato, curry leaves and 250 ml (9 fl oz/1 cup) of water, and cook, stirring regularly, for 6 minutes or until the water has evaporated and the mixture is thick and well combined.

Remove the pan from the heat and remove the dried chillies, season to taste, cool, then refrigerate until firm. Shape the mixture into walnut-sized balls and place on a baking paper-lined tray. Refrigerate for up to 5 days.

For the batter, sift all the ingredients together into a bowl. Stir in 250 ml (9 fl oz/1 cup) of water and whisk until a thick, smooth batter forms.

Heat the remaining oil in a deep-fryer or large heavy-based saucepan to 180°C (350°F) or until a cube of bread dropped in the oil browns in 15 seconds. Working in batches, dip the potato balls into the batter, allowing the excess to drain, then deep-fry for 3 minutes or until golden. Drain on paper towels and serve while still hot.

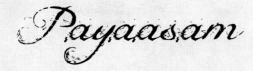

Payaasam

My memories of this dish come from Fiji, not Sri Lanka. Karen and I worked on beautiful Vatulele Island for more than two years and during that time we made some wonderful friends. The construction crew were of Indian descent from Tamil Nadu in southern India and their food was very similar to ours. Once the Indian boys, as they were known, had their own kitchen they cooked all types of food that was very familiar to me. I ate with them regularly and this was always the dessert we had when there was a celebration or festival.

This dish is good hot or cold.

Ingredients

90 g (3¼ oz/⅓ cup) ghee	10 g (¼ oz) dried vermicelli noodles
1 tablespoon cashew nuts, chopped	100 g (3½ oz) caster (superfine) sugar
1 teaspoon raisins	5 green cardamom pods, seeded
200 g (7 oz) sago	and ground
1 litre (35 fl oz/4 cups) coconut milk (see Glossary)	SERVES 6

Method

Heat 2 tablespoons ghee in a small frying pan over medium heat and cook the cashews and raisins for 2 minutes or until the raisins appear toasted. Remove them from the pan and drain on paper towels.

Heat the remaining ghee in a saucepan over medium heat, add the sago and cook, stirring regularly for 7–8 minutes or until the sago is lightly toasted. Add the coconut milk and 500 ml (17 fl oz/2 cups) of water and simmer, stirring regularly, for 10 minutes or until the sago is transparent. Add the vermicelli and cook for 3–5 minutes or until the mixture thickens slightly, then stir in the sugar and ground cardamom and cook for 5 minutes or until the mixture fully thickens.

Serve hot or cold sprinled with the cashew mixture.

MUSLIM FOOD

Although Islamic people make up only about 10 percent of the population they have brought delectable ingredients like rosewater, saffron and cashews into Sri Lankan cuisine. Of course, you won't find pork in Sri Lankan recipes of Muslim origin.

Buriani chicken

This dish is loved by all in Sri Lanka and is considered to be one of the most sumptuous dishes in our cuisine. The best Buriani I have ever had was in the Muslim area of Rangoon in Myanmar.

Ingredients

1 size 16 (1.6 kg/3 lb 8 oz) chicken, meat removed and cut into large pieces, bones reserved

100 g (3½ oz) plain Greek-style yogurt

30 g (1 oz/¼ cup) cashew nuts, chopped

30 g (1 oz/⅓ cup) freshly grated or desiccated coconut

70 g (2½ oz) ghee

½ teaspoon paprika

1 small onion, finely chopped

3 cloves

3 green cardamom pods, bruised

2 cinnamon sticks

100 g (3½ oz/1 cup) basmati rice

1 bay leaf

a pinch of saffron threads

500 ml (17 fl oz/2 cups) chicken stock

BURIANI SPICE MIX

1½ tablespoons coriander seeds

1 teaspoon cumin seeds

1 teaspoon black peppercorns

1 clove

3 long dried red chillies

¼ teaspoon caraway seeds

¼ teaspoon cardamom seeds

SERVES 6

Method

For the buriani spice mix, place all the ingredients in a heavy-based frying pan and dry roast over low heat for 7–10 minutes or until fragrant. Cool, then using a spice grinder or mortar and pestle, grind the mixture until a fine powder forms.

Place the reserved chicken bones in a large saucepan with 2 litres (70 fl oz/8 cups) of water. Bring to the boil over high heat, then reduce the heat to low and simmer for 20 minutes, skimming the surface regularly. Strain, discard the solids and set aside.

Meanwhiile, place the yoghurt, cashews, coconut and 3 teaspoons of Buriani spice mix in a blender and process until smooth. Transfer the mixture to a large bowl, add the chicken and toss to combine well, then cover and allow to stand for 15 minutes.

Heat 1½ tablespoons of ghee in a heavy-based frying pan, add the paprika, half the chopped onion, 1 clove, 1 cardamom pod, 1 cinnamon stick and 1 teaspoon of salt and cook over a medium heat for 5 minutes or until the onion is golden. Remove the chicken from the yoghurt marinade, add it to the onion mix and cook for another 5 minutes. Add the yoghurt marinade and 100 ml (3½ fl oz) water to the pan, simmer for 5 minutes, then transfer the mixture to a large ovenproof dish.

Preheat the oven to 180°C (350°F/Gas 4).

Wash the rice well, then drain. Heat the remaining ghee in a heavy-based frying pan. Add the remaining onion, 1 teaspoon of salt and all the remaining spices except the saffron, then cook for 5 minutes or until the onion is golden. Add the rice, stir until well coated, then add the stock, bring to the boil and simmer for 3 minutes. Stir the saffron threads into the rice, then pour the rice mixture over the chicken. Seal tightly with foil, then a lid. Cook in the oven for 20–30 minutes or until the rice is tender.

Goat curry

This dish traditionally includes the liver and heart of the goat, but it works just as well when tomato paste is substituted for the offal. You can also replace the goat with lamb.

Ingredients

450 g (1 lb) goat or lamb, preferably chump chops with bones

1 goat's liver and heart (optional) or 2 tablespoons tomato purée (concentrated purée if offal not used)

1 small onion, finely chopped

1 sprig fresh curry leaves, leaves picked

1 stick cinnamon

2 garlic cloves, finely chopped

2 thin slices of ginger

10 cm (4 in) piece pandanus leaf

1 lemongrass stem, bruised

7 cardamom pods, bruised

½ teaspoon fenugreek seeds, lightly roasted

1 teaspoon roasted curry powder (see page 36)

½ teaspoon chilli powder

½ teaspoon ground turmeric

1 teaspoon meat curry powder (see page 30)

2 teaspoons ground coriander

1 teaspoon ground cumin

juice of ½ a lime

SERVES 6

Method

Chop the goat (including the offal, if used) into 2 cm (¾ in) pieces, leaving the bone in.

Place all the ingredients in a heavy-based saucepan, add 1 litre (35 fl oz/4 cups) of water and bring to the boil. Simmer for 25 minutes or until the gravy thickens and the meat is tender.

Watalappan

This coconut-based custard pudding is a sweet favourite throughout Sri Lanka.

Ingredients

500 g (1 lb 2 oz) palm sugar (jaggery), chopped

185 ml (6 fl oz/¾ cup) water

a pinch of grated nutmeg

¼ teaspoon ground cardamom

¼ teaspoon ground cinnamon

a pinch of ground cloves

½ teaspoon natural vanilla extract

10 whole eggs

250 ml (9 fl oz/1 cup) coconut milk (see Glossary)

125 g (4½ oz) lightly roasted cashew nuts, chopped

SERVES 4

Method

Preheat the oven to 180°C (350°F/Gas 4).

Place the palm sugar and the water in a small saucepan and stir over low heat until the sugar dissolves, then remove from the heat. Add the spices and the vanilla extract to the syrup.

Lightly whisk the eggs in a large bowl, then gradually whisk in the palm sugar syrup, followed by the coconut milk. Strain the mixture, then pour it into a 1.5 litre (52 fl oz/6 cups) capacity ovenproof dish, and cover tightly with foil. Place the ovenproof dish in a deep baking dish and pour in enough hot water to come halfway up the side. Bake for 15–20 minutes, then remove the foil, sprinkle the cashews over the top and bake for another 15–20 minutes or until just set.

Kottu rotti

This popular dish is commonly served as a filling snack at roadside stalls, or as part of a main meal. The clanging of steel blades chopping rotti is one of my enduring childhood memories.

You will need to make the gothamba rotti in advance.

GOTHAMBA ROTTI

Ingredients

500 g (1 lb 2 oz) atta flour (see Glossary)	1 teaspoon sugar
1 egg	1 teaspoon salt
125 ml (4 fl oz/½ cup) milk	1 teaspoon powdered milk
125 ml (4 fl oz/½ cup) water	3 tablespoons vegetable oil
30 g (1 oz) butter	MAKES 12

Method

Place all the ingredients in a bowl and combine until the dough comes together. Knead on a lightly floured surface for 3 minutes or until the dough is smooth and elastic. Place into a lightly oiled bowl and allow to stand at room temperature for 1 hour.

Divide the dough into 12 portions, brush each one all over with a little oil and place on a tray, then cover with a damp cloth and allow to stand for another hour.

Lightly brush a work surface with oil and roll out each ball into a disc approximately 20 cm (8 in) round. Heat a griddle or large heavy-based frying pan over medium heat and cook the rotti for 30 seconds on each side or until lightly coloured and puffed. Do not overcook as the rotti will become brittle.

KOTTU ROTTI

Ingredients

80 ml (2½ fl oz/⅓ cup) vegetable oil

1 onion, finely chopped

2 garlic cloves, finely chopped

2 teaspoons finely chopped ginger

1 sprig fresh curry leaves, leaves picked

3 long green chillies, finely chopped

1 leek, finely chopped

2 carrots, grated

6 gothamba rotti, cut into 1 cm x 5 cm
(½ in x 2 in) strips

450 g (1 lb) curried chicken, beef or mutton,
drained, chopped and gravy reserved

3 eggs, lightly beaten

SERVES 4

Method

Heat the oil in a large heavy-based frying pan, add the onion, garlic, ginger, curry leaves, leeks and carrots. Season to taste and cook over medium heat for 6–8 minutes or until the onions are soft.

Add the rotti strips and meat and stir for 2–3 minutes or until heated through. Add the beaten egg and stir for another minute or until just set. Serve hot with the reheated reserved gravy.

Sweet
temptations

chapter five

Sweet temptations

RATHER THAN ENDING EVERY MAIN MEAL, SRI LANKAN DESSERTS ARE USUALLY KEPT FOR CELEBRATIONS. WHILE CREAMY PUDDINGS LIKE KIRI BATH (PAGE 126) AND WATALAPPAN (PAGE 191) ARE UNIVERSAL FAVOURITES, THIS CHAPTER OFFERS A SELECTION OF EVERYDAY TREATS AND SPECIAL OCCASION DELICACIES.

Every household had a very large black wok stashed high up in the kitchen rafters for use on special occasions. Our wok and its giant stirrers were too big for the kitchen stove, so once all the ingredients had been bought, we would head outside to prepare the cooking fire.

In a flurry of activity the ingredients would be weighed and chopped under the eagle eye of my grandmother. Luckily for me, my Mum made detailed notes of everything.

All the children would hang around, enthusiastically offering to weigh the sugar and take away the dirty bowls, hoping for a taste of the delicious sweet scrapings and leftovers. The spoon was the greatest prize—my aunties knew they would always have an army of kids willing to stir for hours just to get a lick. Even the men got involved in the festivities, as most of these sweet dishes needed a lot a stirring.

Family celebrations were always so much fun, bringing us all together around the wok, joking and chatting as we cooked.

Wedding cake

This very special and expensive cake is ideal for all special occasions and is made with great pomp and ceremony. I made it with my Mum in November 2007 and she reminded me that as recently as the 1970s no one in Sri Lanka had ovens at home. When baking a cake the ladies of the house had to organise a time with the village baker when they could place their cake in his oven. If you gave the baker a few rupees he would take good care of the cake for you.

Cake tins had to be very well lined with newspaper on the bottom so the heat from the wood-fired oven did not burn the cake.

When this cake is cooked in Sri Lanka, the women sometimes crumble it all up and then push it back together before icing it. Mum and I decided this must have been done to increase its volume and get a better yield out of it.

You will have to plan this cake at least two months in advance as the fruits need to macerate. All the preserves are readily available from Sri Lankan and Indian food stores.

Ingredients

375 g (13 oz) cashew nuts	½ teaspoon ground cloves
375 g (13 oz) sultanas (golden raisins)	55 ml (1¾ fl oz) natural vanilla extract
375 g (13 oz) raisins	55 ml (1¾ fl oz) natural almond extract
500 g (1 lb 2 oz) pumpkin preserve (see Glossary)	30 ml (1 fl oz) rosewater
	300 g (10½ oz) honey
375 g (13 oz) ginger in syrup	200 ml (7 fl oz) brandy
375 g (13 oz) pears in syrup	19 egg yolks
375 g (13 oz) pineapple jam	500 g (1 lb 2 oz) caster (superfine) sugar
175 g (6 oz) strawberry jam	8 egg whites
1 teaspoon ground cinnamon	375 g (13 oz) coarse semolina
1 teaspoon ground cardamom	375 g (13 oz) unsalted butter, chopped

ICING (FROSTING)

900 g (2 lb) icing (confectioners') sugar

30 ml (1 fl oz) natural vanilla extract

30 ml (1 fl oz) natural almond extract

175 g (6 oz) soft unsalted butter

375 g (13 oz) cashew nuts, finely ground

MAKES ABOUT 120 PIECES

Method

Coarsely chop the cashews, sultanas, raisins and preserves and place them in a large bowl or jar with the jams, spices, extracts, rosewater, honey and brandy. Combine well, then seal tightly and refrigerate for 2 months.

Using an electric mixer, whisk the egg yolks and caster sugar until thick and pale, then whisk the egg whites separately until stiff peaks form.

Place the semolina in a dry frying pan and stir over low heat for 8 minutes or until it feels crunchy in your mouth. Make sure the semolina does not burn. Remove from the heat, add the butter and stir until the butter is melted and well combined.

Fold the egg yolk mixture into the macerated fruit mixture, then fold in the semolina and butter mixture followed by the egg whites. Cover the bowl with a tea towel (dish towel) and allow to stand for 1 hour; this will help make the cake denser and more moist.

Preheat the oven to 170°C (325°F/Gas 3).

Line the base and sides of two 8 cm (3¼ in) deep, 25 x 50 cm (10 x 20 in) cake tins with 8 sheets of newspaper followed by greased baking paper. Stir the cake batter well and divide among the tins. The cakes only rise a little so the tins can be filled to just below the top. Cover the tins with foil, then bake for 1½ hours or until a skewer comes out clean. During this time, rotate the tins from top to bottom twice, each time turning them front to back. Cool the cakes in the tins, then turn them out onto wire racks to cool completely. The cooked uniced cakes will keep in airtight containers for up to 6 months.

To make the icing, use an electric mixer to beat the icing sugar, extracts and butter until light and fluffy, then stir in the ground cashews and combine well. Spread the icing over the cake, then cut it into 3 x 6 cm (1¼ x 2½ in) pieces.

Love cake

Delicious with a cup of Ceylon tea, and a lovely treat at Christmas time, this cake probably originates from the Dutch or Portuguese. It has become a national sweet and its recipe, although simple, is hard to perfect.

Ingredients

125 g (4½ oz) soft unsalted butter	1 tablespoon rosewater
125 g (4½ oz/1 cup) fine semolina	1 tablespoon honey
10 egg yolks	¼ teaspoon grated nutmeg
150 g (5½ oz) caster (superfine) sugar	¼ teaspoon lemon rind
150 g (5½ oz) pumpkin preserve, diced	¼ teaspoon ground cinnamon
(see Glossary)	**MAKES ABOUT 30 BITE-SIZED PIECES OR 1 CAKE**

Method

Preheat the oven to 150°C (300°F/Gas 2).

Place the butter and semolina in a bowl and stir until well combined.

Mix the egg yolks and sugar until combined, then add the semolina mixture and combine well. Add the remaining ingredients and combine well. Divide the batter among silicon petit four moulds or spoon into mini muffin moulds. Bake for 8 minutes or until the tops are golden. Alternativly, to make one large cake, pour the batter into a greased and baking paper-lined 6 cm (2½ in) deep, 25 x 50 cm (10 x 20 in) cake tin and bake for 30 minutes or until the top is golden and a skewer comes out clean.

Allow the cakes to cool slightly in the moulds or tin, then turn out onto a wire rack to cool completely.

Halapa

These unique kanda leaf-wrapped sweets are enhanced by the flavour of the leaf. They were one of the most delicious treats we sampled when we were invited into the home of the village baker. I remember his sister making them for us, and that they were still warm when they were served.

The sweet coconut-based stuffing, known as pani pol, is also popular in other dishes, especially string hoppers.

Ingredients

400 ml (14 fl oz) palm treacle (see Basics)	20 kanda leaves, or banana leaves (if using
1 large coconut, split and scraped	banana leaves, trace around a saucer as
½ teaspoon ground cardamom	a guide and cut out 20 rounds)
375 g (13 oz) rice flour	MAKES 20

Method

Put the treacle in a heavy-based saucepan and bring it to the boil. Add the coconut flesh and cardamom and cook over medium heat for 3–5 minutes, stirring continuously. Remove the pan from the heat and stir in the rice flour.

While the mixture is still warm, take a heaped tablespoonful and flatten it out in the palm of your hand to make a disc. Put this on the kanda or banana leaf and fold it in half (the mixture will be a bit like playdough). Place the parcels, flat, in a bamboo steaming basket, cover and steam over a pan of boiling water for 5 minutes, then serve immediately.

Milk toffee

Making this sweet treat was a ritual at our house—everyone got involved because the mixture needed constant stirring. Milk toffee was made for special occasions and we all loved it. Squares would be individually wrapped in coloured paper which had been shredded on the ends—very appealing!

Ingredients

500 ml (17 fl oz/2 cups) coconut milk, either freshly squeezed or tinned (the creamier the better for this recipe)

350 g (12 oz) caster (superfine) sugar

125 g (4½ oz) raw cashew nuts, roughly chopped

5 green cardamom pods, bruised

MAKES ABOUT 20 SQUARES

Method

Put the coconut milk and sugar in a heavy-based saucepan and stir continuously over medium heat until the mixture comes to the boil. Reduce the heat to low, then simmer for 1 hour or until it begins to caramelise, stirring continuously to prevent the mixture from catching.

Add the cashew nuts and cardamom pods and cook, stirring gently until the mixture reaches 126°C (260°F) on a sugar thermometer. Pour the mixture into a lightly oiled baking tin so that it is at least 1 cm (½ in) deep. While the mixture is still hot, cut it into 2 cm (¾ in) squares.

This recipe is pictured on page 198–199.

Coconut rock

This is every kid's favourite and it is easy to make.

Ingredients

200 ml (7 fl oz) milk

750 g (1 lb 10 oz) caster (superfine) sugar

450 g (1 lb) freshly grated coconut

2 drops red food colouring

MAKES ABOUT 30 PIECES

Method

Put the milk and sugar in a heavy-based saucepan, stir over low heat until the sugar dissolves, then bring to the boil. Add the coconut and stir for another 5 minutes or until the mixture reaches 121°C (250°F) on a sugar thermometer.

Divide the mixture into two heat-proof bowls, add the pink food colouring to one bowl and combine well. Pour the white mixture into a lightly oiled baking tin so that it is at least 1 cm (½ in) deep and flatten out, using a lightly oiled banana leaf or the back of a large spoon.

Smooth the pink mixture over the top. Allow to cool slightly and cut into diamonds or squares.

This recipe is pictured on page 198.

Bibikan

This rich coconut- and cashew-based baked cake showcases cloves and cinnamon with a hint of ginger. Bibikan is lovely with a cup of tea.

Ingredients

350 g (12 oz) fresh grated coconut

750 g (1 lb 10 oz) grated palm sugar (jaggery)

150 g (5½ oz/⅔ cup) caster
(superfine) sugar

100 g (3½ oz) plain (all-purpose) flour

175 g (6 oz) cashew nuts, chopped

45 g (1½ oz) crystallised ginger, chopped

1½ teaspoons allspice

1½ teaspoons grated lime zest

MAKES 24

Method

Preheat the oven to 170°C (325°F/Gas 3).

Place the grated coconut in a piece of muslin (cheesecloth) and extract as much milk as possible, then transfer the flesh to a mortar and pound with a pestle until it is pulpy.

Put the coconut milk, palm sugar and caster sugar in a heavy-based saucepan and stir over low heat until the sugar has dissolved. Add the coconut and cook until the mixture reaches 116°C (241°F) on a sugar thermometer and comes away from the sides of the pan.

Remove the pan from the heat, add the flour, cashew nuts, ginger, allspice and lime zest and combine well.

Place 12 lightly greased egg rings on two baking paper-lined oven trays and divide half the mixture among the rings so that each of them is three-quarters full. Bake for 12–15 minutes or until the cakes are firm but moist, rotating the trays halfway through cooking. Cool the cakes slightly, remove the rings, then repeat with the remaining mixture.

Bibikan are delicious warm but are usually served cold. They will keep in a sealed container for up to 1 week.

The bakery

chapter six

The bakery

OUR NEIGHBOURS OWNED THE VILLAGE BAKERY AND THEIR SON OFTEN CAME OVER TO PLAY WITH US. WE WOULD ALWAYS CONVINCE THIS POOR BOY TO BRING SOME OF THE TREASURES FROM HIS ALMIRA FOR US ALL TO PLAY WITH, DESPITE THE FACT THAT HIS DAD WOULD GIVE HIM A HIDING IF HE FOUND OUT. THE ALMIRA IS THE SHOWCASE IN MOST SRI LANKAN HOUSES. ALL THINGS PRECIOUS ARE PLACED IN THERE, MOST OF THEM NEVER TO BE RELEASED. THERE ARE PHOTOS, BOOKS, PLATES, DOLLS, TOY CARS AND ANYTHING ELSE THAT HAS SENTIMENTAL VALUE FOR THE FAMILY.

In 2007 I went back to visit this man and his lovely family; his mother remembered me as the naughty boy who would always get her son into trouble.

The bakery was a fascinating place for me. First thing every morning we watched the bakers loading firewood into the massive eighty-five-year-old original oven and lighting the fire so it would be hot enough for the midnight bake.

We played among the flour bags and chased the rats. When they were caught in traps they were never killed because the bakers were all Buddhists and it was unthinkable to kill anything. Instead, they would take the rats into the bush and release them. The rats always came back. We knew this was true because one of the bakers once put a dab of whitewash on the back of a rat; no matter how far they took it from the bakery it would end up in the trap a few weeks later.

All the different breads came from the same dough. It was an oily, slightly sweet and very yeasty mix. Back in 1968 they were making the dough on the same long wooden bench that had been there from the opening of the bakery decades earlier. Today they still roll and shape the different breads on this old bench.

I vividly remember the process. The flour was poured out onto the bench and shaped into a huge well. Meanwhile, the yeast was mixed with water and toddy and allowed to ferment. At about 9pm all fifteen of the bakers would take up their positions around the bench and a few of the younger boys would pour the yeast mixture into the flour well. Then the bakers would mix and knead the giant dough and leave it to prove. Later, it was broken into many pieces and formed into the sweet, savoury and standard loaves.

At midnight the loaves went into the hot oven and by 3am, the wonderful aroma of freshly baked bread was wafting through the whole village.

The owner of a bakery was always under pressure to supply his village with good bread at the right price and, very importantly, correct weight. We were told that a baker who short-weighed the bread would be punished by being pulled out of his house, stripped naked, tarred and feathered and paraded down the street while everyone shouted insults and laughed. This never happened to our very respectable baker but my Dad explained that this seemingly harsh punishment was designed to save the baker's family from unnecessary suffering: if there was a monetary penalty, the baker would not be able to afford to feed his family.

High top

This is the standard bread; it is light with a crusty top and is the perfect bread to have warm with coconut sambal.

Ingredients

450 g (1 lb) strong flour	250 ml (9 fl oz/1 cup) warm milk
1 teaspoon salt	80 ml (2½ fl oz/⅓ cup) warm water
50 g (1¾ oz) margarine	olive oil, for brushing
10 g (¼ oz) dried yeast	
1 teaspoon caster (superfine) sugar	**MAKES 2 LOAVES OR 12 ROLLS**

Method

Place the flour and salt in a large bowl, then rub the margarine into the flour.

Combine the yeast, sugar, milk and water in a bowl, then add this to the flour mixture and combine until a soft but dry dough forms. You might need to add a little more flour if the mixture is too wet.

Turn the dough out onto a lightly floured surface and knead for 5–7 minutes or until it is smooth and elastic. Place the dough in a lightly oiled bowl and turn it so that it is coated with the oil. Cover the bowl with a damp cloth and allow it to stand in a warm place for 1 hour or until the dough has doubled in size.

Preheat the oven to 200°C (400°F/Gas 6).

Punch the dough down and shape it into 2 loaves or 12 rolls. Place these on a heavy-duty baking tray, brush them with olive oil, dust with a little extra flour and bake for 35–40 minutes or until they are golden and the bases sound hollow when tapped.

Malu paan

These delicious fish-stuffed rolls are especially popular with children and are an essential snack for pre-dawn workers like taxi drivers and fishmongers.

Ingredients

750 g (1 lb 10 oz) strong flour	600 ml (21 fl oz) warm milk
60 g (2¼ oz) suet, finely chopped	1 egg yolk, beaten, for glazing
2 tablespoons caster (superfine) sugar	
1 egg, lightly beaten	**FILLING**
3 teaspoons dried yeast	1 quantity fish cutlets filling (see page 163)
2 teaspoons salt	**MAKES 16 ROLLS**

Method

Put the flour in a bowl, rub in the suet until the mixture resembles coarse breadcrumbs, then add the sugar, egg, yeast and salt and combine well. Gradually add the milk and mix until the dough comes together. Turn it out onto a lightly floured surface, then knead for 5–7 minutes or until it is smooth and elastic. Place the dough in a lightly oiled bowl and turn it so that it is coated with the oil. Cover the bowl with a damp cloth and allow it to stand in a warm place for 1 hour or until the dough has doubled in size.

Meanwhile, divide the filling into 16 portions and shape into balls. Put them on a baking paper-lined tray and refrigerate until needed.

Preheat the oven to 200°C (400°F/Gas 6).

Knock down the dough, then divide it into 16 balls. Working with one ball of dough at a time, flatten it into a triangular shape approximately 1 cm (½ in) thick, place a ball of filling in the middle and fold the edges to form triangular-shaped parcels.

Place the parcels on a baking paper-lined baking tray, brush them all over with the egg yolk and bake for 7–10 minutes or until the glaze starts to brown. The rolls have to be soft, so don't overcook them.

Serve the rolls immediately, or cool and freeze them straight away.

Twisted sugar bread

This is a favourite around the world. Sometimes known in Sri Lanka as kimbula or crocodile bread, in Spain these sweet and slightly oily rolls are called vigilantes.

Ingredients

450 g (1 lb) strong flour	10 g (¼ oz) dried yeast
1 teaspoon salt	115 g (4 oz/½ cup) caster (superfine)
50 g (1¾ oz) margarine	sugar, for sprinkling
2 eggs, lightly beaten	2 teaspoons caster (superfine) sugar
80 ml (2½ fl oz/⅓ cup) warm water	dissolved in 100 ml (3½ fl oz) water
250 ml (9 fl oz/1 cup) warm milk	for brushing
1 teaspoon caster (superfine) sugar	MAKES 25

Method

Put the flour and salt in a large bowl, then rub the margarine into the flour. Add the eggs and stir until just combined.

Combine the warm water, milk, 1 teaspoon of sugar and the yeast, pour into the flour mixture and combine until a soft but dry dough forms. You might need to add a little more flour if the mixture is too wet. Turn the dough out onto a lightly floured surface and knead for 5–7 minutes or until it is smooth and elastic. Put the dough in a lightly oiled bowl and turn so that it is coated with oil. Cover the bowl with a damp cloth and allow it to stand in a warm place for 1 hour or until the dough has doubled in size.

Preheat the oven to 200°C (400°F/Gas 6).

Punch the dough down and break it into 25 tennis ball-sized pieces. Roll each piece out into a 15 cm (6 in) sausage leaving the ends pointy and the centre thick. Using the palm of your hand flatten out the centre in both directions so you are left with a diamond shape. Sprinkle sugar onto it, then in one move roll it into a Swiss roll-style log. Place on a baking paper-lined heavy-duty baking tray, brush with the sugar water, then sprinkle liberally with sugar and bake for 15–20 minutes or until golden.

Wood apple cream

Wood apples are cricket ball-sized pungent fruit whose sticky brown pulp is encased in a very hard shell. When ripe they look slightly mouldy and should rattle when shaken. The flesh is not eaten raw but is best made into a drink or jam.

Wood apple jam is commercially available and is lovely on toast. This drink, in which the wood apple pulp is mixed with freshly squeezed coconut milk, is hard to beat and has a cult-like following.

Ingredients

4 ripe wood apples or 375 g (13 oz) tinned wood apple purée

500 ml (17 fl oz/2 cups) fresh coconut milk (see Glossary)

75 g (⅓ cup) raw (demerara) sugar

juice of 2 limes

MAKES 4 CUPS

Method

Break open the wood apples, scoop the flesh into a bowl and add half the coconut milk. Using your hands, squeeze the mixture together until the wood apple is pulpy. Push the mixture through a coarse sieve, discard the fibres, then add the sugar and a pinch of salt and stir until dissolved.

Add the remaining coconut milk and the lime juice, then strain again through a fine sieve and serve immediately. (You cannot refrigerate this drink as the coconut will separate.)

Wickramapalas favourites

chapter seven
Wickramapalas favourites

I WANT TO DEDICATE THIS LAST CHAPTER TO MY DAD WHO WAS SEVENTY-THREE WHEN HE DIED (07/11/1923–16/8/1997). ALONG WITH MY MUM, HE TAUGHT ME ALL I KNOW ABOUT LIVING WELL.

In my everyday life I still try to follow Dad's teachings on family pride, good judgment, respect for my fellow human beings and life skills. My Mum taught me how to show affection to others as well as to sew, iron, clean up after myself and generally be self-sufficient from a young age.

Dad's time in Australia was hard: both he and Mum were well-educated people—Dad was an engineer and Mum was a qualified Montessori teacher. But when we arrived in Australia they were both told they would have to go back to school. As it turned out, my Dad went to work in an aviation engineering factory. Even though he hated it, he stayed in that job until they had paid off our house—in those days, a grand total of thirty-three thousand Australian dollars.

Dad was an excellent handyman and taught us how to plumb, build, repair cars and sort out electrical problems. Most of the serious and funny conversations I had with my Dad occurred while lying under a car changing a gearbox or doing other repairs. The serious chats would start with him saying, 'Why don't you listen to your mother?'

He had a good sense of humour and a strong sense of pride in the Kuruvita name—he made it clear that if we chose to disrespect his name then we were not

allowed to use it. This was mostly directed towards me as I was the troublesome one; I'm sure my parents spent many a night hoping that their wayward son Peter would come good.

One night, after I had been brought home by the police again, my Dad sat me down and explained to me that I had a choice: to follow one of two paths. The first was to accept the love, support and sense of belonging that were all laid out for me; the other option was to follow the path of a criminal and outcast, in which case all those privileges would be taken away from me—including his surname, as I had not yet earned the right to use it.

The beginning of Dad's death came suddenly: I got a call to say that he was in hospital and that he'd had a stroke. Luckily, all of us were in Sydney and we dropped everything, closed our businesses and rushed to be with him and Mum.

The next five days were intense and amazing. As Dad lay dying in hospital, people came from everywhere—the hospital's rule of only three people in a room was swept aside. Eventually the doctors and nurses moved Dad into a private room so we could be with him all the time. I went to the Blue Mountains and fetched the three Sinhalese Buddhist monks from the temple Dad was affiliated with, and they performed the rituals and ceremony that meant so much to him.

Dad died in our arms surrounded by the people to whom he had devoted his life. For the next three days there was always someone with his body. My brothers and I drank his Scotch and talked, laughed and cried. Mum was never far away. We all celebrated his life and mourned losing our beloved father and husband. It was a sad yet uplifting time. Nothing else mattered except ensuring that the proud head of our family was treated with great respect, even in death.

Mum always says that people are only dead when no one speaks about them any more. We talk about Dad all the time—his body is gone but his spirit lives on in all of us.

Dad was a good cook—he took up cooking late in life when he was semi-retired and Mum was still working full-time. His curries were superb; he was constantly striving for the taste he remembered from his own mother's cooking. You would hear him scream, 'I got it!' when he was able to replicate some of her flavours. He thought that if you did not sweat while eating a curry it was not right—at every meal, at least one of the curries or condiments had to have the fire of the devil in it. He was also adamant that one dish had to be a 'rice puller'—meaning that it was so tasty you could not help but put more rice on your plate to stretch out your experience of that flavour.

His relentless pursuit of recipes and tastes from his mother's kitchen spawned new dishes and these deserve a special mention. Here are four of his best.

Jardi

My Dad called this dish a rice puller—so tasty you keep needing more rice, as you can't stop eating it. Jardi is a curry made from cured, dried fish such as mackerel and tuna, or smaller fish. In Sri Lanka, the small inland boutiques tend to breed small perch or carp in tanks. As the natural flavour of these fish is not so good, they are cured first, and then deep-fried till they are crisp. Then the flavour is wonderful.

I have a curing recipe scrawled on a page from an old exercise book—one of my aunties probably wrote it out in English for my Mum. It calls for 1 measure of rock salt, 3 gallons (about 14 litres) of sea water and half a measure of Goroka. The fish is layered in this mixture and allowed to stand for 1 week. Then the liquid is drained off and the fish is put out in the sun to dry. It's easier to buy it from a spice shop.

My preference is to use mackerel or tuna in this dish. Jardi has a fiery kick and is served as a condiment, so you will only need a teaspoonful per person.

Ingredients

100 g (3½ oz) dried mackerel or tuna, soaked in cold water for 5 minutes

55 ml (1¾ fl oz) vegetable oil

1 onion, thinly sliced

1 garlic clove, thinly sliced

1 sprig fresh curry leaves, leaves picked

3 vine-ripened tomatoes, cut into 2 cm (¾ in) pieces

1 teaspoon dried chilli flakes

½ teaspoon freshly ground black pepper

juice of 1 lime

SERVES 6–8 AS A CONDIMENT

Method

Drain the fish, then cut it into 1 cm (½ in) pieces.

Heat the oil in a heavy-based saucepan or small wok, add the onion, garlic and curry leaves and cook for 8–10 minutes or until the onion is golden.

Add the drained fish and tomato and cook for another 5 minutes or until the tomato is pulpy. Add the chilli flakes and pepper and cook for another 2 minutes. Remove from the heat, stir in the lime juice and season to taste with salt.

Black pepper beef

This dish is so simple and tasty; it is great to eat when drinking arrack.

Ingredients

250 g (9 oz) beef fillet or trimmed sirloin

50 g (1¾ oz/ ⅓ cup) black peppercorns, coarsely ground

1 red onion, thinly sliced

100 ml (3½ fl oz) white vinegar

100 ml (3½ fl oz) vegetable oil

2 small green chillies, thinly sliced

SERVES 6

Method

Slice the beef very thinly against the grain and coat each side with the ground pepper.

Layer the beef slices in a shallow non-metallic bowl, scatter with the onion and sprinkle with ½ a teaspoon of salt. Pour the vinegar over and allow to stand for 30 minutes.

Heat the oil in a heavy-based saucepan over high heat until it is just smoking. Cook the beef slices on each side for 15 seconds, then add the onions and the marinade and cook for another 5 minutes or until most of the liquid has evaporated. Add the chilli, combine well and serve.

Pumpkin curry

Dad's pumpkin curry was a bit unorthodox, but tasty. The original recipe calls for ground mustard seed but Dad used to put in a teaspoonful of hot English mustard instead. This is the way I make it as well.

Ingredients

1 teaspoon raw long-grain rice

2 tablespoons freshly grated or desiccated coconut

1 large onion, finely chopped

1 sprig fresh curry leaves, leaves picked

100 ml (3½ fl oz) coconut cream (see Glossary)

1 teaspoon hot English mustard

500 g (1 lb 2 oz) jap or kent pumpkin (winter squash), seeded and cut into 3 cm (1¼ in) pieces

2 small green chillies, chopped

1 teaspoon Maldive fish flakes (see Glossary)

1 teaspoon ground cumin

1 teaspoon ground coriander

¼ teaspoon turmeric powder

2 garlic cloves, thinly sliced

300 ml (10½ fl oz) coconut milk (see Glossary)

a pinch of roasted curry powder (see page 36)

SERVES 6

Method

Put the rice in a dry frying pan and stir over medium heat until it becomes light golden brown, then remove from the pan. To the same pan, add the coconut, onion and curry leaves and stir for another 5 minutes or until the coconut turns dark brown.

Put the toasted rice and the coconut mixture in a mortar and pound with a pestle until a paste forms. Add the coconut cream and the mustard and combine well.

Put the pumpkin, chilli, Maldive fish flakes, cumin, coriander, turmeric, garlic and the coconut mixture in a saucepan and bring to the boil. Simmer over medium heat until the pumpkin is just tender then, stirring continuously, add the coconut milk and bring to just below the boil. Remove from the heat, season to taste, then sprinkle with a little roasted curry powder and serve.

Devilled beef

This is another hotel speciality. I am not sure of its origins but it seems to be a mix between a Chinese sweet and sour dish and a European stew. It is found on almost every menu in Sri Lanka; or you can request it, as everyone knows how to make it. It is perfect with a cold beer.

Ingredients

60 ml (2 fl oz/¼ cup) vegetable oil

1 onion, cut into 2 cm (¾ in) pieces

1 leek, white part only, cut into
  2 cm (¾ in) pieces

1 sprig fresh curry leaves, leaves picked

2 garlic cloves, thinly sliced

2 banana chillies, cut into thin rings

2 vine-ripened tomatoes, cut into 8 wedges

300 g (10½ oz) beef fillet or sirloin, thinly
  sliced against the grain

2 long red chillies, thinly sliced

60 ml (2 fl oz/¼ cup) Sri Lankan chilli
  tomato ketchup

SERVES 4

Method

Heat the oil in a heavy-based saucepan or wok until it is just smoking. Add the onion, leek, curry leaves and garlic and cook over high heat for 4 minutes, then add the banana chilli and tomato and cook for another 3 minutes or until soft.

Add the beef and red chilli and cook for 3 minutes, then add the chilli tomato ketchup and cook for another 1–2 minutes or until heated through.

Glossary

ATTA FLOUR
This fine wholemeal wheat flour is used in making Indian flat breads. It is generally available from Asian grocery stores. Good quality fine wholemeal wheat flour sold in health food stores can be used as a substitute.

BANANA LEAF
The large flexible leaves of the banana tree are used throughout Asia to wrap foods for steaming or baking. They keep the food moist and impart a mild flavour. To prepare banana leaves for cooking, remove the thick central stalk, rinse the leaves well and blanch them in boiling water so they soften. Lightly oiled aluminium foil can be used as an alternative.

COCONUT
The coconut palm is referred to in Sinhalese as a gift from the gods. Every part of the tree is used—in building, for utensils and as food, right down to the flesh, the cream and the milk. Finely grated in sambals and malums, added as milk or cream to curries and baked into sweet delights, coconut is the quintessential Sri Lankan ingredient.

Desiccated coconut, tinned coconut cream and tinned coconut milk can be bought from Asian grocers and most supermarkets. They are adequate substitutes for freshly grated or shredded coconut, fresh coconut cream and fresh coconut milk.

To crack open a coconut, whack it with the back (the blunt edge) of a large cleaver. Reserve the watery liquid as it drains out, as this can be used in making coconut cream and milk. Scrape out the white flesh, remove the brown membrane, and grate the flesh with a hand grater or in a food processor.

COCONUT CREAM

Also known as first extraction or thick coconut milk, coconut cream has a thick, almost spreadable consistency and is very rich. To make coconut cream, place the grated flesh with the reserved water from a coconut in a blender. Using the pulse action, process until everything is well combined and the flesh is soft. Line a sieve with muslin and place it over a bowl. Pour in the blended coconut, then gather the sides of the muslin and squeeze tightly to extract as much liquid as possible from the flesh. The yield will vary depending on the size and freshness of the coconut. Use immediately, or freeze.

If you use a canned or powdered product, consistency may vary considerably and liquid quantities may need to be adjusted.

COCONUT MILK

To make coconut milk (also known as second extract coconut milk), repeat the coconut cream process (above), using coconut flesh that has already been blended and sieved once. Use filtered water if coconut water is not available. Coconut milk has a much thinner consistency than coconut cream. Use immediately, or freeze.

If you use a canned or powdered product, consistency may vary considerably and liquid quantities may need to be adjusted.

CURRY LEAVES

These small, shiny, pointed leaves from a citrus-like tree native to Asia have a spicy fragrance and are used in southern India, Sri Lanka and Malaysia to impart a distinctive flavour to curries and vegetable dishes. Curry leaves are often fried in oil before being used in curries and chutneys. Although also available in dried form, curry leaves are at their aromatic best when fresh and all the recipes in this book call for fresh.

GOROKA (KOKAM)

A souring and thickening agent unique to Sri Lanka, goroka is a fluted orange fruit whose segments are dried, turning black. It can be soaked in hot water and ground to a paste or added whole and removed after cooking. It is most commonly used in fish curries such as ambul thial. Goroka is available from Asian grocers and specialist spice outlets.

KANDA LEAVES

Kanda is an Ayurvedic herb, said to be good for digestion. Like banana leaves, kanda leaves are often used as wrappers for steamed or baked. They are available from Asian grocers.

KANG KUNG

Also known as water spinach, kang kung is a leafy vegetable that is readily available from Asian grocers. The leaves have a mild flavour and add a vibrant green colour to curries.

MALDIVE FISH FLAKES

Maldive fish flakes are made in the republic of Maldives from skip jack tuna, and are produced in three stages—boiling, smoking, then sun-drying. They have the same importance in Sri Lankan cooking as shrimp paste does in Thai, Indonesian or Malay cooking. Used sparingly in most Sri Lankan curries as a thickening agent, they are a key ingredient in pol and seeni sambols, and part of the secret to achieving an authentic Sri Lankan flavour. They have a strong aroma and a lovely smoky flavour. Maldive fish flakes can be kept for up to a year, stored in a sealed glass jar.

MURUNGA

Also known as drumsticks, murunga has a long, ridged dark green pod with a slightly bitter flavour. It is a popular ingredient in vegetable curries, particularly kiri hoddy and white curry. Discard the outer skin after scooping out the pulp in the soft centre.

PALM TREACLE

Also known as panni, palm treacle is produced from the juice of the kittul palm flower. The end of the flower is cut off and an earthenware pot is placed over it to catch the juice. This juice is boiled until thick and then smoked, producing the syrup with its delicious, unusual flavour. Palm treacle is a key ingredient in the national treat called 'curds (yoghurt) and honey'. Fermented palm treacle is called toddy and can be used as a raising agent instead of yeast.

PANDANUS LEAVES

Most Sri Lankan households grow the pandanus plant, the long green leaves of which are used to perfume curries and rice. Pandan (also known as rampe) is often referred to as the vanilla of Asia, such is its beautiful aroma. Available fresh or dried from Asian grocers.

PUMPKIN PRESERVE

Coarsely grate flesh of 450 g (1 lb) ash pumpkin or hairy melon. Put pumpkin in a tea towel (dish towel) and secure with kitchen string. Hang over a bowl for 2 hours to drain off any liquid. Put 675 g (1 lb 8 oz) caster sugar and 120 ml (4 fl oz) water in a heavy-based saucepan and bring to the boil. Add pumpkin and cook on medium heat, stirring regularly to prevent mixture from catching, for 10–15 minutes or until it begins to leave the side of the pan and reaches 121°C (250°F) on a sugar thermometer. Add 1 teaspoon rosewater and 2 drops yellow food colouring, combine well. Pour mixture in a greased 23 x 30 cm (9 x 12 in) tin, smooth the top and let cool. Cut preserve into 2 cm pieces and store in an airtight container for up to 6 months at room temperature. Makes about 120 pieces.

SAMBA RICE

This pungent country rice is the standard rice in Sri Lanka. The grains are tiny—my Mum used to call them chicken teeth.

Index